# HEIDEGGER AND WHITEHEAD

# HEIDEGGER AND WHITEHEAD

*A Phenomenological Examination
into the Intelligibility of Experience*

By  Ron  L.  Cooper

Ohio University Press
*Athens*

Ohio University Press books are printed on acid-free paper ∞

97  96  95  94  93      5  4  3  2  1

**Library of Congress Cataloging-in-Publication Data**

Cooper, Ron L.
    Heidegger and Whitehead : a phenomenological examination into
the intelligibility of experience / by Ron L. Cooper.
       p.    cm. — (Series in continental thought ; 19)
    Includes bibliographical references and index.
    ISBN 0-8214-1060-1 (alk. paper)
    1. Whitehead, Alfred North, 1861-1947. Process and reality.
2. Heidegger, Martin, 1889-1976.  Sein und Zeit.  3. Phenomenology.
4. Experience.  I. Title.  II. Series.
B1674.W353P7632     1993
113—dc20                          93-21562
                                      CIP

To Bruce Wilshire
for placing me within the right horizons
and to my wife Sandra
for keeping them bright

# CONTENTS

## PREFATORY NOTE

Martin Heidegger's *Being and Time* can be broadly termed a transcendental inquiry into the structures that make human experience possible. Such an inquiry reveals the conditions that render human experience intelligible. Using *Being and Time* as a model, I attempt to show that Alfred North Whitehead's *Process and Reality* not only aligns with *Being and Time* in opposing many elements of traditional Western philosophy but also exhibits a similar transcendental inquiry. With this reading, *Process and Reality* contains concepts much like Being-in-the-world, ecstatic temporality, and others found in *Being and Time*. Most important, this interpretation considers Whitehead's treatment of human experience paradigmatic for understanding his cosmological scheme in general. Finally, the results of this study are employed to sketch a phenomenology of holy experience.

# 1

# *Introduction*

A LFRED NORTH WHITEHEAD'S *Process and Reality* (PR) and Martin Heidegger's *Being and Time* (BT) may have inspired more philosophical publications in the twentieth century than any other books.[1] It might seem, then, that these two great works would invite comparison. While the books appeared only two years apart (*Being and Time* in 1927, *Process and Reality* in 1929) and the men were but a generation apart (Whitehead born in 1861, Heidegger in 1889), the two thinkers wrote quite independently, each apparently unfamiliar with the other's work. On the surface, *Process and Reality's* legacy of process thought and the existential phenomenology that grew from *Being and Time* seem to be quite disparate. The view that these two philosophical approaches share no kinship persists in spite of Calvin O. Schrag's short essay of thirty years ago that sketches the common ground found in these two great philosophers. In addition, although the work of some process thinkers, such as Schubert Ogden, exhibits substantial influence from existentialism, no more than a few paragraphs here and there comparing Whitehead and Heidegger can be found.[2]

Whitehead's and Heidegger's analyses of experience are perhaps most readily contrasted in the view that Whitehead interprets human experience as an instance of his causal theory of nature (which some readers see as old-fashioned metaphysics), while Heidegger offers a transcendental description of human existence (which strikes some readers as too subjectivistic.) A causal account of nature is certainly important to Whitehead's cosmology, and he remarks that in regard to offering explanations of what is at work in process, the most fundamental principle could even be referred to as "the principle of efficient, and final causation" (PR 24). Indeed, process is often characterized as the coming to be of events out of their influences upon one another, the creative advance occurring in the appropriation of past reality and the transmission of this reality into future potential. And while a full account of human existence must include the recognition of causality in our world, it is true that Heidegger's description of the essential features or transcendental structures of human being makes almost no mention of causality.

I wish to show that Whitehead can be read as offering a description of human experience that can more or less be viewed as a paradigm for understanding other sorts of events. When we examine Whitehead's approach to the question "How do we discover causal categories?" the causal features of Whitehead's notion of human experience can be seen as transcendental structures of experience, that is, those features that render intelligible the possibility of any experience at all and not as categories taken from a theory of causality and then imposed upon human experience. Heidegger's transcendental analysis is one of phenomenologically exposing the primordial "existentialia" of experience, the conditions without which our experiences cannot be understood to be possible. It is my view that in the manner that Heidegger describes the existentialia that make any experience possible, Whitehead shows that we come to an understanding of causality not through a scientific inquiry into efficient causes but through an analysis that reveals the primordial *Ereignis* of causality to be a structure of originative experience itself. Working through Heidegger's method of excavating these existentialia in *Being and Time* equips us with an interpretive scheme by which we can discover a similar transcendental analysis operating in *Process and Reality*.

The essence of this method is captured in Whitehead's remark that "the aim of philosophy is sheer disclosure."[3] Through this approach of disclosure, we are able to formulate a worldview so that "every element of our experience can be interpreted" (PR 3). These innocent statements become peculiar when Whitehead continues by saying that "our datum is the actual world, including ourselves; and this actual world spreads itself for observations in the guise of the topic of our immediate experience" (PR 4). Although Whitehead's concern for disclosing the immediate content of experience certainly reveals at least an alignment with the goals of phenomenologists, a number of questions are raised: Is it not question-begging to interpret experience by a method created from that very experience, especially if we include ourselves as experiencers? Why is the actual world said to be in the "guise" of experience? If we recognize a certain experience as immediate, why are we in need of a method to disclose it? Whitehead writes that we have no "clear-cut complete analysis of immediate experience" (PR 4) and insists throughout his work that immediate experience, though lively, is vague. His responses to these questions become clearer as we understand what he means in saying that "the problem of philosophy is to discriminate exactly what we know vaguely,"[4] and the content of this vague knowledge is immediate experience. The task, then, is to make intelligible our immediate experience so that we can discover how it is possible to have any experience of the actual world.

Similarly, Heidegger's lifework is a search for the meaning of Being, a term for which we all have only a vague understanding in spite of our seeming familiarity with it (BT 19). The method for clarifying this vagueness is what Heidegger calls "phenomenology," which, Schrag says, "in its broadest intention, is an attempt to return to the immediate content of experience, and to analyze and describe this content as it actually presents itself."[5]

Both Heidegger and Whitehead recognize that the attempt to describe the immediate content of experience is *part* of this content and that the struggle to bring to awareness what was originally unreflective contributes to the vagueness that we are trying to overcome. The two thinkers develop self-criticizing methods that unfold through the course of transcendental analysis the attempt to render intelligible the conditions that make human experience possible.

Central to their methods is the contention of both Heidegger and Whitehead that traditional epistemology is mistaken in taking self-reflecting, conscious events to be our most immediate experiences. They reject a priori epistemological theories that focus upon intellectual activity at the expense of the phenomena themselves. Schrag writes that for Heidegger the "datum or phenomenon of existence is always prior to any epistemological theories concerning it."[6] On this point, Whitehead agrees that "consciousness presupposes experience, and not experience consciousness" (PR 53). However, "the whole universe consists of elements disclosed in the analysis of subjects" (PR 166). It is important to note from the start that Whitehead does not use the term *subject* in the same sense that philosophers ordinarily use it, and unfortunately he is sometimes sloppy in distinguishing his peculiar uses. Whitehead has more to say about consciousness than does Heidegger, and when we understand that experience extends far beyond the conscious realm, we may agree with Whitehead that consciousness "makes us human. But it does not make us exist."[7] So, to understand human existence, we must clarify our given, immediate experience, but immediate experience does not, as we often believe, always involve reflective awareness.

The key to elucidating what is given in immediate experience lies in the referential, intentional nature of worldly affairs. What is given in experience is not a set of objectified, actual facts, for we find the given *as* "referent to an external world, and in this sense will be said to have a 'vector character'; it involves emotion, and purpose, and valuation" (PR 19). Whitehead finds the given as charged with potential for feeling; indeed, the term "'Potentiality' is the correlative of 'givenness'" (PR 44). Understood in the sense of vectors, experiences are always feelings *of* . . . , valuations *of* . . . , and the given is always potential *for*. . . . We are fundamentally involved in the world because of the intentionality basic to our involvements. Whitehead writes:

The basis of experience is emotional. . . . The occasion as subject has a 'concern' for the object. And the 'concern' at once places the object as a component in the experience of the subject, with an affective tone drawn from this object and directed towards it. With *this* interpretation the subject-object relation is the fundamental structure of experience.[8]

A hint of Whitehead's treatment of the subject-object relation is found in the above passage. The affective tone drawn from and directed toward the object in the vector of experience are not two separate activities for Whitehead, for the presence of the object resonates within the experiencer. The "subject-object relation is the fundamental structure of experience" *only when* understood as two poles of the same event. The fact that this event is basically emotional and not basically intellectual, as will be shown later, is what undercuts substantialist dualism. The above passage could be extracted almost verbatim from *Being and Time,* for Heidegger says that the Being of human existence is care *(Sorge).* "Care" is Heidegger's term for the fundamental intentional structure of human being, an existence that always finds itself situated in the midst of a relational context. The relations in this context are, as with Whitehead, more affective than cognitive.

Since we are never outside of concrete, relational situations, our understanding of this experience must take the total context into account. As Hubert L. Dreyfus and Stuart E. Dreyfus write, both Heidegger and Whitehead accuse traditional philosophy of "focusing on facts in the world while 'passing over' the world as such. This means that philosophy has from the start systematically ignored or distorted the everyday context of human activity [and has assumed a world of] context-free elements."[9] Whitehead warns that "the understanding of the immediate brute fact requires its metaphysical interpretation as an item in a world with some systematic relation to it" (PR 14). To rely upon our conscious representations of the world while forgetting our emotional and practical involvements in it may lead us to view the world as composed of context-free elements. But we must notice that elements which shine with immediate distinctness, in some circumstances, retire into penumbral shadow in other circumstances, and into black darkness on other occasions. And yet all occasions proclaim themselves *within* the flux of a *solid* world, demanding a *unity* of interpretation. (PR 15; stress added)

It is a mistake to suppose that we can neatly isolate the given as if we were visually separating the colors and textures of a painting and then examine those elements by means of easily articulated categories of the intellect. Of course, something is given in experience, but it is not added to the experience like a new brick to a wall. The given appears more like a thread woven into, blending into, giving strength to, and expanding the experienced world. To have an experience is to weave a thread into (perhaps *be* a thread in) a universe that is pulsating and growing into space-time.

Heidegger finds that the intellectual separation of any object from its relational context removes the "worldliness" of the object, that is, the possibility of an intentional unity found in our concrete involvements. The ability to involve ourselves with objects, to experience the world, presupposes relations of experienceability. We intend an entire field of possible involvements in each act of experiencing an element of the world. To consider any particular involvement to be an isolated fact is to make an abstraction in which we ultimately ignore the experiential features that we meant to examine in the first place. So philosophical interpretation must begin before the "facts," in the world in which we already have a vague understanding of the objects' relations.

I do not mean to suggest that either Whitehead or Heidegger maintains that we cannot coherently speak of individual experiences. Indeed, we come to understand the experienceable world in general through explicating what we find in concrete, particular events of experience. But for both thinkers, "to understand" *means* to uncover the experiential matrix of possible relations surrounding any given "fact." Thus, the possibility of understanding is progressively revealed in terms of what the understanding enables us to understand. The circularity of this approach is apparent.

In Elizabeth M. Kraus's companion work to *Process and Reality,* the following passage applies equally to Heidegger:

> In [Whitehead's] view, a fact is understood when it can be placed in a wider systematic context which gives an account of its interconnections with other facts. . . . The true activity of understanding consists in a voyage to abstraction which is in fact a voyage to the more fully concrete: to the system in which the fact is enmeshed. The system as *conceptualized* may be more abstract than the fact itself in that it is more general, but the real systematic context is more concrete, and its elaboration yields more about the existential relations of the fact.[10]

Giving a systematic account of experience amounts to moving from the particular event to the wider situation in which the event is possible, back to a finer analysis of the event, and then back to an expanding matrix of relations. In this manner, we make transcendental progress by asymptotically approaching but never fully reaching a perfect degree of articulation. Although Heidegger clearly makes use of this method, it is sometimes hidden in Whitehead, perhaps because of his misleading tendency to catalog his categories as if he were about to offer a logical proof. The purpose of this essay, however, is to show that a study of Heidegger's use of this method will illuminate Whitehead's use of a transcendental analysis of experience.

It is particularly evident in Heidegger that the circularity involved in *explaining* the possibility of experience is also found in *having* experiences. For Heidegger, the understanding is primarily a structure of human existence and secondarily a faculty of the reflective intellect. Understanding the world is part of that "concern" that Whitehead (quoted above) says the "subject" has for the "object." Without some understanding of the world, we could not care for it; without caring for the world, we could not experience it. Each experience occurs within the context of our care for the world and is thus an instantiation of our "care-ful" interpretation of the world. Existentially concerned for this contextual world in which we are emotionally involved, we cannot but interpret experience in terms of that concern. In this way, not only philosophical analysis but experience itself involves, indeed is, hermeneutics. This hermeneutical character of experience will be explored presently, but now it is important to see that this notion goes hand in hand with Heidegger's and Whitehead's transcendental approach to making the possibility of experience intelligible and with their opposition to a philosophical tradition that has focused upon substance and its subsequent emphases upon subject-object and subject-predicate constructions.

In his approach to the Being question, Heidegger calls for the "destruction of the history of ontology" (BT 44), which begins as far back as ancient Greek thought. But the crux of disclosing our embeddedness in the experiential world lies in seeing that in the modern "tradition the decisive *connection* between *time* and the *'I think'* was shrouded in utter darkness; it did not even become a problem" (BT 45). Descartes's treatment of the cogito as a detached, thinking subject ignores the self's unique, historical existence. For Heidegger, the self is always Being-in-the-world, never apart from the field in which it is situated or its temporal movement that makes that field possible. Human being, or Dasein, *means* the self as well as its historical situation. This characterization can be grasped only when the ego-subject of Descartes is abandoned.

Whitehead calls this egoistic view of the experiencing self the "evil produced by Aristotelian 'primary substance' " that leads to subject-object and subject-predicate formulations, which are only modern substitutions of primary substance (PR 30). The dualism inherent to Descartes's thought is "in-coherent" (PR 6), little improved upon by Spinoza's monism, which clings to a substance-quality conception (PR 7). Descartes's dualism leads directly to a representational theory of perception (PR 49) by which "orthodox philosophy can only introduce us to solitary substances, each enjoying an illusory experience" (PR 50). Any such "notion of an unessential experience of the external world is entirely alien" to Whitehead, for he "interprets experience as meaning the 'self-enjoyment of being one among many, and of being one arising out of the composition of many' " (PR 145).

Whitehead laments Descartes's near-miss when the "I think" is seen as an *event,* an act of experience taken to be the primary type of human existence. However, "like Columbus who never visited America, Descartes missed the full sweep of his own discovery, and he and his successors, Locke and Hume, continued to construe . . . experience according to the substance-quality categories" (PR 159). Heidegger is in full agreement, and he claims that Kant, whose transcendental analysis is so close to Heidegger's, committed a similar mistake in neglecting to include the world *in* experience.[11] Kant was correct, according to both Heidegger and Whitehead, in insisting that philosophy should examine the transcendental structure of experience instead of the transcendental structure of ("external") reality. But Kant, as well as three centuries of his predecessors, treated perception as if it were "a process of returning with one's booty to the 'cabinet' of consciousness after one has gone out and grasped it" (BT 89). On the contrary, when human being "directs itself towards something and grasps it, . . . it is always 'outside' itself alongside the entities it encounters" (BT 89). Heidegger's notion of human being as "outside itself," that is, as "ecstatic" existence that can never be simply located in space-time, will provide an important concept for Whitehead as well.

The tendency of philosophers who follow Descartes in examining the cogito but leaving unexamined the *sum* (BT 46) results in the "assumption that the basic elements of experience are to be described in terms of one, or all, of the three ingredients, consciousness, thought, sense-perception" (PR 36). Whitehead has much more to say than Heidegger about the conscious elements of experience, but he considers consciousness a higher form of experience whose basic nature is a positive or negative selectivity. An understanding of conscious functions comes only after an analysis of how it grows out of the more basic elements of experience; otherwise we suffer from not noticing how "the selective character of the individual obscures the external totality from which it originates and which it embodies. . . . The task of philosophy is to recover the totality obscured by the selection" (PR 15). Examining immediate experience necessarily involves some sort of conscious separation. It is this separation of given elements that obscures the related and embodying ingredients of the experience without which any particular element becomes only an abstraction. Without a method of description that seeks to keep the entire experience intact, we mistakenly take conscious representations of the world "out there" to be the true objects of inquiry.

Both Whitehead and Heidegger recognize that the primacy given to consciousness, representational epistemology, and subject-predicate and substance-quality constructions is deeply entrenched in Western thought and language. Perhaps the attempt to overcome this entrenchment accounts for the extraordinarily difficult language of *Being and Time* and *Process and Reality*. The reader of these works must constantly keep in mind that he or she most likely assumes substantialist answers to follow from questions of reality, experience, and self; does not ordinarily think that a subject-predicate proposition should be "considered as expressing a high abstraction" (PR 138); does not regard human experience, as Theodore Kisiel writes, as referring "at once to the experiential process of disclosure and the field of relations in which man is implicated";[12] and does not describe himself or herself, as F. Bradford Wallack writes, as "primarily emotional and not primarily conscious, or ideational, or knowledgeable, or perceptive."[13] John E. Smith summarizes the view that is central to Western thought, and he points out the opposition to this view by Heidegger, Whitehead, and kindred thinkers:

> The experience to be given up is the one which says that experience is a tissue of subjectivity of which we are immediately aware, a veil which stands between ourselves and the world so that it is possible to claim that experience is "merely" some inner state which, though it may have some sort of psychic existence,

does not disclose any reality beyond it. But this is precisely the conception of experience which has come under attack from the phenomenologists, the pragmatists and the existentialists, not to mention the tradition represented by Bergson and Whitehead.[14]

I wish to show that *Process and Reality* and *Being and Time* are very similar in purpose. The fundamental agreement between the two works is explicit in the titles: the authors share a basic intuition that all of reality is essentially temporal. Whitehead did not write of process on the one hand and reality on the other, nor did Heidegger mean to distinguish Being and time as separate domains of study. It is creative process that makes reality possible for Whitehead, just as time is the disclosive ground of Being for Heidegger. Moreover, it is their nonlinear characterization of time by which real entities are better understood as events than substantial objects that allies the two philosophers against nearly the whole of the modern philosophical tradition. Heidegger's ecstatic temporality of Dasein and Whitehead's epochal concrescence of the actual occasion provide the basis for an interpretation of reality in which the past is absorbed into the real constitution of things as projected futurally for a dynamic unity. Both thinkers find this temporal kinesis that flows through the very heart of Being displayed most vividly in human experience, which thereby becomes, as Husserl would say, a *Leitfaden* or transcendental clue for an interpretation of Being as such.

Our experience is more emotional than intellectual, more active involvement than passive observance. We are not receptive, private subjects that mirror external objects; we can perceive only because we are always in the midst of those perceivable events. Whitehead's and Heidegger's view of human experience as a concerned engagement in a network of worldly events is grounded in a doctrine of intentionality fundamental to our existence. Although Western philosophy has repeatedly considered the world a collection of isolated facts that we try to make coherent by epistemological theory, Whitehead and Heidegger find such coherence in the intrinsic referential character of both experience and its data. For both thinkers, a philosophical method devoid of ego-object, sub-stance-quality, and subject-predicate dualities allows the tem-poral and spatial intentionality in experience to reveal itself.

This work will attempt to do more than just expose com-mon themes in Heidegger's and Whitehead's works; it will try to show that an understanding of ecstatic temporality de-scribed in *Being and Time* provides a phenomenological approach that helps to reveal the intentional structure of ex-perience as found in *Process and Reality*. I readily admit that there are important limitations to this Heideggerian reading of Whitehead's works. In spite of their similarities, as Schrag reminds us, in the end "Heidegger thinks historically and voluntaristically; Whitehead thinks scientifically and cosmo-logically."[15] Nevertheless, this interpretation should be useful in divining phenomenological and transcendental currents in *Process and Reality* that may otherwise remain unearthed.

As Heidegger is concerned in disclosing no less than what it means to *be,* Whitehead wishes "to frame a coherent, logical, necessary system of general ideas in terms of which every element of our own experience can be interpreted" (PR 3). A critical point is made here in Whitehead's characterization of the purpose of his speculative philosophy. Although *Process and Reality* offers a cosmological account of reality, *it is the interpretation of our own experience that guides the devel-opment of his metaphysical system,* and Whitehead writes in *Adventures of Ideas* that *Process and Reality* endeavors to show that the structures by which we interpret our "imme-diate present occasion of experience" can be directly applied to our interpretation "of all occasions in nature."[16] Thus, we can anticipate thematic similarities to *Being and Time* that arise from the effort to provide a transcendental account of experience.

Heidegger's description of the way human existence finds itself in a world of existential involvement and takes up its his-torical situation can be applied to Whitehead's treatment of experience as composed of an absorption and projection of the past. Also, Heidegger's insistence upon the primacy of the future bears upon Whitehead's notion of internal process, or concrescence, which directs entities toward a fulfillment of particular experiences. Specifically, Whitehead's "system of general ideas" by which we interpret our experience exhibits phenomenological features much like Heidegger's existentialia: Whitehead's "actual occasions," his term for experiential events that are the ultimate constructs of the universe, are characterized by an intentional openness much like Heidegger's Being-in-the-world; as Being-toward-death guides Heidegger's Dasein toward its temporal wholeness, each actual occasion has a "subjective aim" toward its own end. Actual occasions reveal, like Dasein, a historicality by which they "prehend" or appropriate the past and project this appropriation futurally. These prehensions occur within "subjective forms," that is, unique interpretations of the world in terms of the actual occasions' particular situatedness, much as Dasein's experiences are colored by moods. And the actual occasion's primary and concrete involvement with the world, which Whitehead calls "causal efficacy," provides the possibility for more abstract understanding, operations that allow rough but interesting comparison with Heidegger's derivation of *Vorhandenheit* from *Zuhandenheit*.

This work, perhaps unfortunately, will proceed at times in a manner somewhat like those of *Being and Time* and *Process and Reality*. Neither of those works develops in a step-by-step presentation: important concepts surface briefly and repeatedly resurface to be explicated further each time. As best as can be managed, there is a linear development to this study, but even the styles of the two books reflect the referential context of events and the nonlinear nature of temporality to such a degree that they nearly demand a commentator to explicate the whole of either work all at once. Thus, I beg the reader's patience with incomplete explanations that should become fuller later in the book.

The final chapter is a sketch of a phenomenology of what will be called holy experience. There are special, deeply personal experiences that I think give a coherence to our existence. Heidegger's and Whitehead's work show how we can discover the temporally and spatially unifying structures of these holy experiences. Although the work as a whole is a study of how the two thinkers attempt to make intelligible the possibility of any experience, the phenomenological sketch of these holy experiences suggests one way it may be possible to find an overall coherence to our entire range of experiences.

# 2

# *Methodology*

*B*EING AND TIME is often criticized as full of sound and fury, a truncated work that hardly approaches fulfilling what it promises. Heidegger is sometimes seen as filled with hubris for claiming to inform the world of the meaning of Being, sometimes as foolish for writing volumes on a vacuous term. But even in making these charges, his critics acknowledge the awful brilliance of his work, his keen insight into his philosophical heritage, and his limitless passion, if not naiveté, to correct what he believed were centuries of a grand intellectual mistake. While bowing to his predecessors, especially Kant, Kierkegaard, Nietzsche, Dilthey, and Husserl, he wrote dozens of works that view the history of Western thought as a magnificent dirge in which the very question that first inspired the ancient Greeks fades further and further from memory. In *Being and Time,* Heidegger reminds us of the question of the meaning of Being but warns that the very asking is a long and hard labor.

Heidegger claims that we all are engaged in a prethematic asking of the question—indeed, we cannot but ask. Human being, as the entity Dasein, is the entity that "includes inquiry as one of the possibilities of its Being" (BT 27). If we can "make an entity—the enquirer—transparent in his own Being" (BT 27), an answer will come to what makes it possible to inquire. The possibility of the inquirer qua inquirer is grounded in Dasein's unique temporality. Here we see the relationship between Dasein and the Being question, for "the fundamental ontological task of interpreting Being as such includes working out the *Temporality of Being*" (BT 40). This inquiry is Dasein's particular mode of being (BT 26–27), and Dasein can inquire about Being only because of Dasein's prethematic understanding of temporality.

Dasein may view its temporality in either of two general ways: a linear series of undifferentiated "now-moments" or a finite, unified event. This latter view is what Heidegger calls "authenticity," in which Dasein understands itself as "historized" by gathering up events it inherits from the past and stretches between birth and death to become a whole self. In the inauthentic view of itself, Dasein is merely an uncollected scattering of events. This notion of authentic Dasein is crucial for Heidegger, for it is only when Dasein has its "own" time that it is able to grasp the meaning of Being.

Underlying the analysis of *Being and Time* is the presupposition that "to be" always means "to be in time." Hence, the Being question can be restated as "How is it that anything at all is in time?" But to ask the question properly is to know how one can be in time in a way to inquire into Being. To understand how one is in time in this way is to understand how Dasein's temporality temporalizes itself. Existing in this manner, Dasein is "open" to Being. Here we see a certain progression in Heidegger's thought, for in his later works he focuses upon this openness to Being more than upon temporality. It is in *Being and Time*, though, that this formulation first arises.

I shall not be concerned with the relationship between the so-called earlier and later Heidegger. The point here is that Heidegger views the temporality of Dasein as the critical idea in getting at the meaning of Being. We shall see that Whitehead also believes that the proper understanding of, the proper response to, temporality is essential to the examination of how anything exists and that the temporality of human experience is paradigmatic.

In his search for the meaning of Being, Heidegger uses the German infinitive *Sein,* "to be." This sense is easily overlooked by English speakers who ordinarily use the term as a gerund and hence think of particular beings *(Seiende)*. However, philosophers writing in other languages (and in German) have also, according to Heidegger, missed this active sense of *to be* and thereby incorrectly conducted their ontological inquiries. In viewing Being as if it were a being, two millennia of thinkers have made the worst category mistake of all, or as Whitehead would say, have been guilty of committing the fallacy of misplaced concreteness. Biologists and physicists conduct experiments and theorize on the nature of beings without questioning the metaphysical bases of these analyses, but the philosopher must provide the foundation for all ontic inquiries by going beyond beings to the ontological question "How is it possible for anything at all to be?"

The distinction between ontological *(ontologisch)* and ontical *(ontisch)* matters is crucial to Heidegger. A similar distinction is made between existential *(existenzial)* and existentiell *(existenziell)* concerns as applied to human existence. An existential inquiry into the ontological structure of human existence discloses universal conditions called existentialia. Existentialia are ontologically prior to the existentiell matters of particular, contingent acts or decisions. My understanding of the French Revolution is a particular, existentiell fact about me that I might not have come to have, but my ability to have any understanding of that concrete series of historical events is an existential structure of my existence. In the same way that "Being is always the Being of an entity" (BT 29), though, existential analysis can never be cut off from the concrete, existentiell facts of what is analyzed.

In his claim that an existential analysis "lays bare" what we already understand ourselves to be, we see Heidegger's special sense of a priori. All of Heidegger's favorite terms of which he claims we have a vague and limited awareness—"fallenness," "Being-in-the-world," and so on—are a priori characteristics in need of clarification. These structures are not a priori in the sense of mental constructions known before or without concrete, possible experience in the world but in the sense of being presupposed *in* the actual experience. Also, Schrag points out that existentialia can be considered transcendentals, for they "are present in the concrete existence, providing its very condition for being, but at the same time they lie beyond every particular instance of concrete existence. All knowledge of the structure of human being is therefore transcendental knowledge."[1] Similarly, for Whitehead, the vague but fundamental feelings of efficacy in the lived body provide a dim awareness of the movements of process.

While these descriptive concepts have universal application, they are not to be applied in the same manner as the traditional notions of categories. For Heidegger, categories *(Kategorien)* apply only to nonhuman beings (BT 70). Substance, relation, quality, quantity, and so on were thought by philosophers to be present in all entities encountered in the natural world and could be used as models for human beings. Philosophers have often been motivated by the need to find a place for human beings in the cosmological order and have found that place by means of categorial definitions such as "rational animal." While such a genus-species construction may contain informative value, Heidegger rebels against any classification of human being that overlooks its historical nature. Human being can never be reduced to an instance of a natural object but must be understood in history; never a substance existing in itself but always an event that stands out from itself toward its historical possibilities; and never a object to be defined but a dynamic occurrence of self-definition.

Only within this characterization of human being can Heidegger's phenomenological method be grasped. In its broadest sense, phenomenology describes the data of immediate experience. It is the most radical empiricism, but traditional empiricists have treated human experience as if it were ahistorical and thereby have misread, according to Heidegger, their data as poorly as their rationalist counterparts. The key to allowing phenomena to present themselves as they really are lies in an appeal to the ancient Greek etymology of phenomenology as *phainomenon* and *logos,* terms that indicate that this method is a science of phenomena ( *Wissenschaft von der Phänomenen,* BT 50. ) Derived from the Greek *phainesthai,* "to show oneself," phenomena can be understood as that which shows itself. The Greek term was closely associated with *ta onta,* "that which is." Thus, phenomena are things that show themselves as they are.

It is obvious that things can show themselves or appear in different ways. An object may even appear as something it is not. A confusion lies in the practice of making synonyms of *phenomena* and *appearance (Erscheinung)*. An automobile problem may "appear" in the form of black exhaust, or an illness may "appear" in certain symptoms. But the black exhaust is not the worn piston rings themselves, nor is a sneeze the allergy. Strictly speaking, neither the worn rings not the allergy has appeared, for they were only signified in the appearance of symptoms.

Also, appearances can mean that which issues while the creator of the issue is not revealed. In this case, there is a "mere appearance" in the form of an effect. The use is found in Kant's treatment of *Erscheinung* as the objects of intuition. These appearances are the correct objects of epistemological investigation for Kant, yet they are at the same time the effects of a noumenal reality that hides itself behind those appearances. But a mere appearance for Heidegger is always the appearance *of* something, something that can, given the correct method of analysis, show itself as itself. Heidegger's elaborate discussion of the different meanings of appearance (BT 51–55) is meant to isolate the sense of phenomenon proper to an ontological study. A phenomenon is not simply an appearance but that which shows itself forth as itself, and all the other meanings of appearance are derivative of and made possible by this fundamental sense.

Turning to the concept of logos, Heidegger reminds us that Plato and Aristotle used the term in a variety of ways, all arising from its basic meaning, "speech." This reference to discourse is covered up in modern translations of *logos* as "account," "reason," "ground," even "cause." Heidegger points out that Aristotle often used *logos* in terms of making manifest what the discourse is about and thus described the function of speech as *apophainesthai,* that is, to let something be open to sight. Speech makes manifest what is spoken about as *apo-*

*phansis* in "vocal proclamation in words" (*Sprechen,* BT 56). Apophantic discourse has the property of synthesis, not in the sense of "a bringing and linking together of representations" but in the phenomenal sense of "letting something be seen in its *togetherness [Beisammen]* with something—letting it be seen as something" (BT 56). Apparently, Heidegger takes the phrases in this latter quotation to be equivalent: apophantic discourse reveals that nothing exists in isolation. This notion of Being as context will prove fundamental to Whitehead too.

As "letting something be seen," logos provides the possibility of truth and falsehood. Truth lies in bringing to light what is hidden in discourse by allowing that which is spoken about to reveal itself in its uncoveredness. Truth for Heidegger is *aletheia;* to speak the truth is to dis-cover. By the same token, falsehood consists in covering up, in hiding something so that it is not revealed as that which it is. We tend to think that truth is "something that 'really' pertains to judgment," but Heidegger says that this is a misunderstanding of the (Greek) concept of truth (BT 57). Truth fundamentally resides in *aesthesis,* "the sheer sensory perception of something" (BT 57). The purest sense of truth, then, applies to pure *noein,* "the perception of the simplest determined ways of Being which entities as such may possess, and it perceives them just by looking at them" (BT 57). At this point, Heidegger's language becomes misleading if it is not kept in mind that the enterprise of phenomenology is to develop this special kind of looking, for what is immediate is not necessarily obvious.

With the discussions of phenomena and logos, Heidegger can bring these terms together and offer the meaning of phenomenology as *legein ta phainomena,* or better, *apophainesthai ta phainomena:* "to let that which shows itself be seen from itself in the very way in which it shows itself from itself" (BT 58). This formal construction, however, does not indicate the phenomena that this method is supposed to bring to light. What is that which phenomenology is supposed to let us see? Heidegger's answer: anything whose nature does not easily show itself but precisely for that reason demands to be allowed to show forth. But this hidden nature that is covered up by what appears "belongs to it so essentially as to constitute its meaning and its ground" (BT 59). What can remain covered up, show itself deceptively, or return to hiding "is not just this entity or that, but rather the *Being* of entities" (BT 59). Thus, phenomenology is the method of ontological inquiry, for *phenomena* always refers to the Being of beings and is not to be constrasted with *noumena* but with un-dis-closedness.

This implicit allusion to Kant is quite revealing. Heidegger understands Kant as considering the Being of a subject's experience of objects to lie in objectivity. J. L. Mehta explains that for Kant,

> the objectivity of objects is an a priori determination and condition of the possibility of all experience of objects. Hence the method by which we pass beyond objects to their objectivity, their Being, is called by Kant transcendental. . . . The transcendental method . . . aims actually at disclosing the ontological structure of essents (conceived by Kant in the narrow, specific sense of objects), that is their Being, and for this reason Heidegger seized upon it as ideally appropriate to his own task of penetrating into man's ontological constitution.[2]

Heidegger's phenomenology can be said to be an extension of Kant's transcendental analysis, but with a twofold difference. First, as already discussed, phenomena can never be separated from the things in themselves, Kant's noumena. Second, transcendental understanding does not occur in the subjective consciousness but is a structural feature of human existence as openness to Being.

Although taking his cue from Kant, Heidegger owes a much larger debt to his mentor Edmund Husserl and his rallying call *"Zu den Sachen selbst!"* (to the things themselves). The "things," of course, are the phenomena that show themselves. The maxim demands that no philosophical theories can form the starting point for ontological analysis. For Husserl, this means that we must suspend belief in, put into "brackets," everything we ordinarily take for granted in experience so that we cast our phenomenological sights upon consciousness itself. If done with sufficient rigor, phenomenology may be established as a strict science of presenting the things themselves, unsullied by epistemological theory and metaphysical presumption.

Husserl's great contribution to philosophy is his investigation into the intentionality of conscious acts. His concern begins with what he sees as the incompleteness of phenomena: that which shows itself needs to show itself *to* something. That to which phenomena are shown is the transcendental consciousness, which is not to be confused with the empirical consciousness that is the object of psychological study. The transcendental consciousness, whose very essence is to be conscious *of* something, in turn relies upon phenomena as that toward which consciousness aims, that which consciousness goes out for, that which consciousness intends. Husserl takes this intentionality to be the basis of consciousness, and in some of his writings, "intentionality" and "transcendental" tend to be used interchangeability. Even in Husserl's characterization of conscious intentionality we see a kinship with Whitehead's notion of the vector character of experience: The experiencer aims at the data even as the data aim at the experiencer.

To explore this intentional structure of consciousness, Husserl attempts to develop a method to reveal the complex contents of consciousness as clearly as we experience a simple sense perception. But even a sense perception comes to us amid a lifetime of assumptions and beliefs about the cause and context of the perception. Husserl tries to work out a step-by-step series of phenomenological or eidetic "reductions" in which reality, as presented in our "naive" experience, is bracketed in hopes of bringing forth the structures that constitute phenomena. Husserl finds that the uniqueness of consciousness lies in the fact that the phenomena are "constituted" by conscious activities regarding the phenomena's essences (or meanings).

Husserl does not mean to say that things are imaginary inventions. Entities are not created by consciousness, but their essences are constructed from the *hyle,* the stuff presented to the synthetic character of transcendental consciousness. Husserl describes these activities as meaning intentions of consciousness and fulfilling intentions of phenomena. For example, my awareness of my desk is not identical to the desk itself. The desk is solid, rectangular, and several feet wide, but my idea of the desk possesses none of those qualities. Although the hardness and size of the desk cannot physically enter my consciousness, they are somehow presented to me from the stuff of my idea of the desk. Husserl shows that this presentation is an exceedingly complex activity in which sense data take many forms and occur within a complicated array of potential sensations. But these sense data would be meaningless without the meaning intentions, the noetic activity of consciousness that assigns appropriate categories such as substance, quality, and explains the relations as the shape, size, of a material object; that is, noetic activities constitute the "whatness" of what is intended by consciousness.[3] For Husserl, the character of truth proposed in any judgment, then, is the agreement of what is meant and what is given in fulfilling intentions.

The difference between Husserl's transcendentalism and Heidegger's is found in the latter's attempt to express the way phenomena are constituted in terms deeper than Husserl's transcendental consciousness. Husserl's attempt is far too idealistic, subjectivistic, and egoistic for Heidegger. In considering consciousness to provide the fundamental, presuppositionless beginning of philosophy, Husserl places himself squarely within the Cartesian tradition[4] that takes the cogito to be prior to what Heidegger considers the ontological structure beneath, the *sum*. Husserl maintains the subject-object dichotomy in just the way Descartes so severely separated *res cogitans* and *res extensa*.

Husserl, of course, goes far beyond Descartes in attempting to resolve how the activities of the knowing subject become connected to the known through the synthetic acts of intentionality. But Heidegger maintains that there is a level of encounter that is ontologically prior to the subject-object construction. Knower-known dualism is an abstraction that arises after, indeed is derived from, the primordial experience of the world in which we find ourselves. To exist is to be intentionally related to the world in a manner that is fully revealed only when the Cartesian point of departure is turned around to establish a "new ontologico-phenomenal confirmation. The *'sum'* is then asserted first, and indeed in the sense that 'I am in a world' " (BT 254).

In this focus upon the *sum* that understands itself in a world, we see the difference between Husserl's notion of a timeless, abstract ego and Heidegger's concept of historical, concrete human existence. The facticity of the conscious subject is never the "pure" consciousness that Husserl claims synthesizes phenomena but arises from an historical situation that is always temporally, logically, and ontologically prior to any Cartesian subjectivity. Husserl unquestioningly presupposes an inarticulated mode of being of consciousness itself. For Heidegger, the being of consciousness must indeed be sought, but this search is possible only after the being of that which is conscious is revealed.

Further for Heidegger, this prior investigation will reveal that intentionality is found in, transcendence placed in, the entity that is conscious and not that entity's consciousness. Human existence intends in *all* its worldly affairs, not just its conscious activities; it transcends even in *existing* alongside other entities, not just when thinking about them. The world is primordially intended not just in judging and perceiving but in driving a car, sawing a plank, carrying on a conversation. The world is primarily transcended not in conscious acts but in a human being's manner of existing *as* the entity that can make ontological inquiries. Human beings exist by means of ecstatic temporality, so that we are always "open" to historical possibility: intentionality is a function of our in-timeness.[5]

Conditioned by facticity, human being presupposes its inherited historical situation in all the possible ways of understanding itself and its world. Heidegger substitutes a hermeneutic of factual existence for Husserl's transcendental phenomenology. Mehta describes this interpretive approach "as the Kantian transcendental method modified and widened under the influence of the more sophisticated discipline of phenomenology and liberalized by an assimilation into it of the 'hermeneutic' procedure of the human sciences *(Geistewissenschaften)*."[6]

Preliminary phenomenological sketches must therefore be verified by returning to experiential facts as concretely exemplified, which in turn are reexamined. This circling movement is present throughout *Being and Time* as Heidegger slowly proceeds to offer descriptions, seek phenomenological meanings, and reinterpret the original descriptions to offer deeper meanings. This hermeneutic spiral in which the inquirer finds itself cannot be avoided, since its subject matter, the Being of beings, tends to alternate from concealment to disclosure and back. Since the inquirer is essentially historical, it must conduct the inquiry from its unique, contextual perspective, or within "horizons." Hans-Georg Gadamer writes:

> We define the concept of 'situation' by saying that it represents a standpoint that limits the possibility of vision. Hence an essential part of the concept of situation is the concept of 'horizon'. The horizon is the range of vision that includes everything that can be seen from a particular vantage point. . . . to have an horizon means not to be limited to what is nearest, but to be able to see beyond it. . . . Similarly, the working out of the hermeneutic situation means the achievement of the right horizon of enquiry.[7]

The right horizon for Heidegger, the limiting vantage point that nevertheless acts as a springboard beyond its own boundaries for uncovering the existential structures buried in a worldly experience, is the temporal, historical situatedness of human being.

The horizons for the inquiry into the meaning of Being surround human existence, for it is in human existence that Being is an issue. Heidegger calls human existence Dasein, from the German *da,* "there," and *sein,* "to be." The dissection of this term provides insight into Heidegger's special use of it: the Being of Dasein is "there" in the sense of "already there," or "already in its manner of Being." To have its Being as an issue for itself *is* the manner of Dasein's Being. Dasein's "guiding activity of taking a look at Being arises from the average understanding of Being in which we always operate and *which in the end belongs to the essential constitution [Wesensverfassung] of Dasein itself"* (BT 27-28). The question of Being is not an issue that Dasein may or may not consider—Dasein always exists in a relation toward Being that provides a pre-ontological, unthematized understanding of Being by which the question may be *explicitly* raised (BT 36). Heidegger's technical use of *Dasein* emphasizes this peculiar, ontological questioning of human being through whose unique, temporal horizons Being may be brought into view.

It is important to note the interrelation of Dasein's preontological understanding of Being and its capacity to question Being. Dasein's preontological understanding is meant in a very pedestrian way. We go about the business of being in a world before we understand clearly what that being is. We conduct ourselves, we are able to encounter beings, within a preconceptual comprehension of Being by which we are ever conditioned without being especially aware of it. We function by an unreflecting notion of Being, taking for granted that things are, unaware that our most familiar experiences are exceedingly difficult to articulate and little troubled that the most mundane events in life are hard to explain. But this vague, unexamined comportment with beings provides the very possibility (which we sometimes choose to explore) of a deeper understanding of what it means to be. This preontological understanding provides a path that points the way to what is, at some times more vivid than others, an issue for us. If ordinary, average understanding suggests a closeness to Being, then to exist as an inquirer illuminates how far we are from clear understanding and how in need we are of a method to guide the inquiry.

Phenomenological hermeneutics finds in Dasein the horizons of temporality that may reveal the *aletheia* of Being. This unconcealment could never take place in the timeless, transcendental consciousness or in the groundless cogito, but must come to light in the historical process that is Dasein.

# Whitehead's Method

WHITEHEAD IS CERTAINLY NO PHENOMENOLOGIST. The most important features of his cosmology—actual occasions, eternal objects, and God—are not directly available to phenomenological investigation. Furthermore, Dasein is not an actual occasion or even properly a series of actual occasions. Thus, any attempt at a systematic comparison of *Process and Reality* and *Being and Time* is seriously limited. Nevertheless, Whitehead approaches much of his project by a transcendental analysis similar to Heidegger's exposition of the structures of human existence that make the possibility of experience intelligible. Just as Heidegger discovers ecstatic temporality to be Dasein's intentional openness toward its world, the very basis of creative process for Whitehead depends upon the actual occasion's ability to appropriate into its constitution the reality of past events and in turn project that reality to future occasions. While real events are actual occasions for Whitehead, the paradigmatic case for this openness is the human experient that literally feels its worldly involvement in the gross body. In this manner, Whitehead goes to the things themselves, prethematic feelings of Being-in-the-world, and then proceeds to offer metaphysical accounts of causality, time, and space.

Although Whitehead considers our vague feelings of appropriations of worldly involvement paradigmatic, *Process and Reality* does not proceed by means of a linear, logical development. Instead, as Donald W. Sherburne points out, the reader "will encounter a weblike development that presupposes the whole system at the very beginning and recurs again and again to individual topics that 'in each recurrence, these topics throw some light on the scheme, or receive some new elucidation.'"[8]

Whitehead considers this hermeneutic approach to his subject matter more appropriate than the explanatory function of argument. In dealing with concrete issues, Whitehead assumes the posture of the phenomenologist whose aim is to describe rather that to justify. Although explanation and argument are ingredients even in the work of Husserl and Heidegger, the nature of the subject matter determines the method of its account, and the "explanatory purpose of philosophy is often misunderstood. Its business is to explain the emergences of the more abstract things from the more concrete things" (PR 20). Briefly, then, "philosophy is explanatory of abstraction, and not of concreteness" (PR 20).

Whitehead's goal of providing a system of general ideas by which our own experience can be interpreted amounts to developing a set of abstract yet precise categories that can render intelligible our concrete yet vague experience. Since the categoreal scheme is abstract, explanatory argument is appropriate. But the method of argument for those categories includes reference to evidence found in the descriptions of concrete experience. *Process and Reality* proceeds in this hermeneutic circle: The first part elaborates a list of categoreal terms and principles providing the general character of process. Next, these principles are considered in the context of certain philosophical issues and the way previous thinkers have made use of them. Then descriptions of concrete, nonconscious experiences and (as we shall see) their derivative cognitive operations bring those principles into focus. Next, the more fully developed scheme is shown to provide systematic treatments of time and space. Finally, equipped with a grand cosmological system, Whitehead offers a rather romantic and somewhat poetic discussion of the philosophy of organism. All along, Whitehead shows that when "we attempt to express the matter of immediate experience, we find that its understanding leads us beyond itself" (PR 14).

Whitehead's ultimate goal is to present a picture of the universe that is not a collection of material objects in various relationships but a rhythmic organism, a dancing plurality of mutually modifying creative events that interrelate and interpenetrate into a unified ever-renewing process. Schrag points out that Whitehead shares Heidegger's notion of *Verweisungszusammenhang* (referential togetherness).[9] All events are related in a deep togetherness that Whitehead expresses as "the category of the ultimate" by which the "many become one, and increased by one" (PR 21).

The "advance from disjunction to conjunction" (PR 21) occurs by

> two kinds of fluency. One is *concrescence* which, in Locke's language, is the 'real internal constitution of a particular existent.' The other kind is the *transition* from particular existent to particular existent. This transition, again in Locke's language, is the 'perpetually perishing' which is one aspect of the notion of time; and in another aspect the transition is the origination of the present in conformity with the 'power' of the past. (PR 210)

This fecund passage captures the essence of process and illustrates the intentionality of the togetherness of events. Open to its past in the same way that Dasein retrieves possibilities from Dasein-that-has-been-there, the actual occasion appropriates its own content from actual-occasions-that-have-been-there. This repetition of past possibility, reinterpreted in accordance with the particular actual occasion's intentional subjective aim toward its end, can be compared with Dasein's retrieval of possibility from having-been, which is always guided by Being-toward-death. As Dasein's Self is the wholeness attained in this process, the actual occasion aims at a synthesis of its appropriated prehensions into a wholeness that Whitehead calls "satisfaction." This side of process is concrescence.

The source of an actual occasion's prehension is its factical relation to the world that arises from possibilities transmitted from past actual occasions. This passing of possibilities is the side of process called transition, and it illustrates two kinds of intentionality in addition to the actual occasion's "internal" intentionality toward its satisfaction:

1. The actual occasion's openness to its past. In its facticity, Dasein finds itself with certain characteristics already inherited, and its historical nature allows it to appropriate its heritage. As the existentialia are necessary manifestations of Dasein's ecstatic temporality, the actual occasion's appropriation and concrescence of past possibilities are necessary features of an

entity in process. While these features may be described, Whitehead says that "there can be no explanation of this characteristic of nature."[10]

2. The passing down of an actual occasion to another. Dasein itself does not exist after death, but the possibilities that were Dasein may be passed on to another. Whitehead's twist upon this occurrence is his position that during its concrescence, an actual occasion is not actual but becomes actual only after it has perished. Upon its completion, the actual occasion becomes part of the givenness of the world, which is then incorporated into other actual occasions. To say that this process of self-creating concrescence is not actual is, in a sense, close to Heidegger's stress upon Dasein's potentiality over its actuality, its existentiality over its facticity. The perished actual occasion achieves "objective immortality" as the data of future actual occasions' experiences, much as the possibilities of Dasein-that-has-been are available to succeeding Dasein.

By the intentional openness of actual occasions, Whitehead can say that "in a certain sense, everything is everywhere at all times."[11] The preposterousness of this statement is reduced when we understand that Whitehead is involved in a struggle to overcome a tradition in which "some chief notions of European thought were framed under the influence of a misapprehension" ( PR 61 ). Western thought suffers from a great mistake that "consists in the confusion of mere potentiality with actuality." The truth is that "continuity concerns what is potential; whereas actuality is incurably atomic" ( PR 61 ).

Each actual occasion becomes what it is through its response to the totality of what has gone before and upon its perishing is potentially *in* all succeeding actual occasions. In appropriating into its constitution elements from its past, the actual occasion is said to have positive prehensions of that experiential data. What is not taken into the actual occasion's constitution is said to be negatively prehended, and these negative prehensions are as essential to concrescence as positive prehensions. Since having the quality of not-A is a description that is just as relevant as having the quality of B, and since these features are real, internal ingredients in the actual occasion and not mere external relations, there is a universal continuity among all events.

This continuity, made possible by the actual occasion's openness to prehend other actual occasions, demands comparison to Dasein's fundamental involvement with the world. It is not the case, for Heidegger, that a carpenter takes a hammer into his Being, but in his *involvement* with the hammer, the carpenter *is,* in a sense, the concernful activity of projecting the potentiality of the hammer onto the event of hammering. When the hammer is considered apart from this context, the hammer is removed from the matrix of its worldhood and is seen as merely present, actual, and atomic. The carpenter's involvement with the potentialities of the hammer is possible only to an entity that is open to the entire world of involved relations. Thus, the ecstatic nature of Dasein allows the carpenter (although this is admittedly stretching the comparison) to be "everywhere" in the worldly matrix of involvements.

Although the actual occasion's spatiotemporal extendedness is ecstatic in such a way that its potentiality allows it to be said to be everywhere, we must not forget that it always occurs in a particular perspective. Whitehead's contention that any reality must occupy a particular "place" is termed the "ontological principle," and he expresses this principle in a number of ways: "Everything is positively somewhere in actuality, and in potency everywhere" (PR 40). Any event "has its reason *either* in the character of some actual entity in the actual world of that concrescence, or in the character of the subject which is in the process of concrescence" (PR 24). "There is no going behind actual entities to find anything more real" (PR 18). "No actual entity, then no reason" (PR 19).

To explain means to point to a concrete event, but there are no reasons why any actual occasions exist, only descriptions of those actual occasions. To say that actual occasions exist because they are instances of creative process is to commit what Whitehead calls the fallacy of misplaced concreteness, that is, to mistake the abstract for the concrete. The cosmic creative process occurs *because of* the openness of actual occasions that makes possible concrescence and transition. There is no further explanation.

Here we see an important difference between Heidegger and Whitehead. It is true that Heidegger examines Dasein in order to come to an understanding of the meaning of Being and that Whitehead forms his categoreal system from the facts of actual occasions. In *Being and Time,* Dasein's openness, its ecstatic temporality, leads the way to an understanding of Being (although this quest is not completed in *Being and Time*). But Heidegger also indicates that his projected work intends to offer an account of why anything at all, including Dasein's ecstatic temporality, exists. Whitehead, on the other hand, may not think that an answer to the meaning of Being is possible.[12] Actual occasions occur, but these occurrences are fundamental in the strict sense.

In spite of Heidegger's larger enterprise, the published portion of *Being and Time* succeeds in describing what it is to experience the world. Dasein is thrown into a world with which it is essentially involved, past possibilities are taken up and projected futurally, and so on. Whitehead's account of the functions of the actual occasion provides a similar description. Elizabeth Kraus explains:

> "To experience" for Whitehead is to synthesize a given multiplicity into a private unity; to be a subject is to be the focus of that experience; "to decide" is to select those aspects of the manifold unifiable from that focus. "To enjoy" is to exist as a unity self-created out of the manifold; "to be satisfied" is to have eliminated all indeterminations as to what that existence might be and thus to have become an "object"—a superject— added to the manifold and given for the future.[13]

It is my view that Whitehead's transcendental analysis of experience has been overlooked in favor of characterizing *Process and Reality* as an account of causal cosmology in which human experience is merely an instance of universal causal relations. My aim is to apply *Being and Time* to *Process and Reality* to allow us to explicate what Whitehead means in writing that the "philosophy of organism aspires to construct a critique of pure feeling, in the philosophical position in which Kant put his *Critique of Pure Reason*" (PR 113). Whitehead does not mean that Kant's analysis of pure reason was wholly successful, for he says that Kant provides a transcendental analysis in mentalistic terms "and therefore conceives of his transcendental aesthetic to be the mere description of a subjective process" (PR 113). Given Whitehead's focus upon the vague feelings of our worldly appropriations, "Kant's 'Transcendental Aesthetic' becomes a distorted fragment of what should have been his main topic" (PR 113).

In a certain sense for Whitehead every event is an experience. That which experiences is not a *thing* that has experiences but a *perspective* for experiencing. Although Whitehead sometimes speaks of actual occasions (or actual entities)[14] as occupying perspectives, he is better understood to say that actual occasions *are* those perspectives or ways of experiencing, as Heidegger is better understood to say that Dasein is a way of existing than that Dasein is an existing thing. To come to grips with Whitehead's extraordinarily complex account of process, it will be helpful to present a brief sketch, in largely uninterpreted technical terms to be explained later, of how actual occasions become.

Like Heidegger, Whitehead places great stress upon potentiality over actuality. Every past actual occasion is a potential datum for a present actual occasion. But to feel is always to feel in a particular way, and potential ways of feeling are called "eternal objects" by Whitehead. The source of these potentials is the special actual occasion God. God retains the traditional role of creator by luring the emerging actual occasion with an eternal object that when selected, determines the way the actual occasion feels the initial datum of its experience. (Whether God determines which eternal object is selected by the emerging actual occasion is a matter of great debate among Whitehead scholars, and I shall attempt no answer to the problem here.) This original selection of an eternal object becomes the actual occasion's subjective aim that guides the actual occasion's experiences throughout its concrescence.

This initial stage of concrescence involves the actual occasion's conformal feelings in which past actual occasions are prehended and appropriated. These prehensions are called "physical feelings," and since they are felt within the actual occasion's unique perspective determined by its subjective aim, they are prehended in a novel way, unlike any before. Guided by the subjective aim, the uniquely felt prehensions are said to occur in *subjective* forms; that is, they are felt as the actual occasion's own. Although physical feelings occur in subjective forms, they are felt as coming from the originative past actual occasions. This is Whitehead's sense of the vector character of prehensions; actual occasions "feel what is *there* and transform it into what is *here*" (PR 87). While certain data are decided upon as positive constituents of the forming actual occasion, others are refused and are termed "negative prehensions." This is not to say that some events are totally unrelated to the actual occasion, for the actual occasion's perspective is characterized as much by what it does not prehend positively as by what it does.

There is a conceptual, though not necessarily conscious reproduction of each physical feeling. The subjective form of a physical feeling takes place by the selection, in accordance with the subjective aim, of an eternal object that becomes the way the feeling is felt. While much is said of Whitehead's Platonism in this regard, for Whitehead, it is better to say that potentials (eternal objects) participate in or ingress into real entities than to say, with Plato, that real entities participate in potentials (Forms). In physical feelings, eternal objects become immanent in the concretion of the temporal world. In conceptual feelings, on the other hand, these potentials are felt as transcendent, that is, as pure potentials available for determination of the definiteness of actual occasions. In this way, physical feelings are conceptually reverted in what Whitehead calls the "mental pole" of concrescence.

The actual occasion integrates its multitude of physical feelings and their conceptual reproductions by the complex functions of transmutation. Collections of actual occasions are found to exhibit a common quality and are said to form a nexus (plural, nexūs). In one manner, a particular eternal object is chosen to exhibit one way of feeling the nexus. For instance, a nexus may be felt "redly." The redness of the feeling becomes the datum for experiencing the entire nexus. In another manner of transmutation, that of simple comparative feelings, the entire nexus is felt as one entity. It is important to remember, however, that nexūs are derivative from the actual occasions that compose them, for to take a rock to be ultimate rather than the multiplicity of events that compose the rock is to commit the fallacy of misplaced concreteness.

From comparative feelings come higher forms of experience leading to consciousness. The datum of a simple comparative feeling is the comparison between a physical feeling and its conceptual reproduction. The conceptual side of this contrast is a potential, while the physical side is an objectified, past occasion. Such a contrast amounts to Whitehead's notion of a proposition: The past actual occasion prehended is the subject of the proposition, and the eternal object involved in the conceptual reversion is the predicate, or predicative "pattern" for Whitehead. Thus, even propositions are understood only in the context of potential experience, for they are said to be lures for feeling the world in some possible way.

An even higher form of feeling occurs in the contrast between a proposition and a nexus. Whitehead calls such contrasts "complex comparative" feelings, or "intellectual" feelings. Although these higher sorts of feelings occur in the mental pole of the actual occasion, consciousness is only one kind of subjective form, and it occurs extremely rarely. Whitehead coins phrases such as "perceptive propositional feelings" in his exceedingly complicated analysis of consciousness, but it cannot be overstressed that for Whitehead, feelings, experiences, and their mental pole are not to be equated with conscious activity. In Heidegger we shall see that Dasein's projection of involvements with worldly experiences takes place in understanding and that Dasein's situatedness always occurs in some mood. While it is tempting to interpret these accounts in terms of consciousness, Heidegger insists that these features are preconscious structures of existence occurring logically prior to any cognitive content about them. Although I can certainly be conscious of my involvements to some extent, my existence as Being-in-the-world as such is not a conscious activity. The same is true for Whitehead. Only a tiny fraction of the total number of actual occasions ever experience in the subjective form of consciousness, and even then, those conscious prehensions depend upon hosts of unconscious feelings.

The series of physical and conceptual feelings develops *toward* the actual occasion's completion. When the subjective aim is fully realized, the actual occasion is said to achieve satisfaction. The actual occasion then perishes with this fully determinate feeling of satisfaction. Whitehead maintains that concrescence is not a temporal series but the happening of an irreducible epoch of process. The actual occasion prehends only actual occasions that have previously perished, and a concrescing actual occasion is the prehended data of only future actual occasions after its own perishing. Although concrescence perishes, the actual occasion remains forever as objective immortality. The epochal actual occasion is an atomic moment through which funnels the power of Being interpreted from a unique perspective.

In working through Whitehead's "system of general ideas in terms of which every element of our experience can be interpreted," we shall see that the actual occasion is characterized by a temporal openness that allows for Being-in-the-world much like Dasein's care. This fundamental intentional openness makes possible the sort of experience that we speak of in ordinary terms. In a letter to a friend in 1939, George Santayana provided a wonderful metaphor for Whitehead's view of experience:

> He asserts (a great truth!) that [ideas] are superficial lights on a great dark ocean of existence. Our animal nature, and all nature, is at work beneath. They, the ideas, are like bell-sounds heard coming from the engine-room when a steam-boat stops or goes full steam ahead. The passenger, the spirit, learns very little from them about the ship, the crew, or the voyage. . . . The ideas, though superficial when clear, when confused are the very heart and substance of the universe.[15]

# 3

# *The Experience of Worldhood*

F OR BOTH HEIDEGGER AND WHITEHEAD, our experiences occur within the context of a world of experienceable events. To understand how our experiences are possible—that is, to conduct a broadly conceived transcendental inquiry that uncovers the experienceability of the world—we must discover what sort of world we find ourselves in. For both thinkers, the world appears to us as an interrelated matrix of events in which we are primordially involved, and it is only derivatively a collection of objects to which we are related as knowers, in the traditionally philosophical sense, to the known. Heidegger's description of the world occurs within his avowed search for *veritas transcendentalis* (BT 62), and Whitehead's use of such notions as eternal objects certainly shows that he is not merely involved in an empirical investigation toward a so-called causal metaphysics.

## *Being-in-the-World*

HEIDEGGER WRITES, *"The essence of Dasein lies in its existence"* (BT 67). "Existence" *(Existenz)* is not used here in the traditional sense of presence but in the special sense of *ex-sistence* that stresses the way "these entities in their Being, comport themselves toward their Being" (BT 67).[1] Dasein's essence cannot be captured by use of a category such as thinking or talking animal, as noted earlier. Thinking and talking are particular possibilities of Dasein, but the aim of Heidegger's analysis is to disclose the ground that allows all of Dasein's possible ways to be. Dasein *is* its possibilities and is always beyond itself as it happens to exist in particular ways, for Dasein is always at access to other possible ways to exist, even when denying them. This accessibility is due to Dasein's essential constitution of Being-in-the-world.

Heidegger speaks of the "inhood" of Dasein, but not in the same sense that a chair is in the room or water is in a glass. It is true that we are at any given moment in a city or in the country, on land or at sea. Each of these situations is an ontic characteristic discovered empirically and by which we can be said to occupy some point on a space-time graph. But such treatment is a categorical way of discussing our physical bodies and not the a priori translocational feature Heidegger intends. In an all too characteristically puzzling etymological derivation harking back to *innan* and *habitare,* Heidegger claims to show that "'ich bin' . . . means in its turn 'I reside' or 'dwell alongside' the world, as that which is familiar to me" (BT 80). His philological indulgences aside, Heidegger's meaning is clear: For Dasein to be *in* the world is to be *with* the world, to be in relation to other entities, to find itself in a complex of possible enterprises.

The world in which Dasein is found is not an enumerable totality of natural objects. Nor does *world* mean particular realms within this totality, such as the world of mathematics. Another sense is our existentiell use of the term, as in "the world of the farmer." The sense Heidegger is interested in at this point is "worldhood," in which the "worldliness" of entities is revealed in their relations to Dasein as utensils. Dasein's possibility of encountering objects as tools indicates the intentionality of Dasein's "inhood." Hubert L. Dreyfus and Stuart E. Dreyfus write:

> Like Wittgenstein, [Heidegger] found that the every-
> day world could not be represented by a set of context-
> free elements. . . . When we use a piece of equipment
> like a hammer, Heidegger said, we actualize a skill
> (which need not be represented in the mind) in the
> context of a socially organized nexus of equipment
> (which need not be represented as a set of facts).
> This context, or world, and our everyday ways of skill-
> ful coping with it . . . forms the way we are.[2]

Dasein's familiarity with the world as a matrix of utensils Heidegger calls "readiness-to-hand" *(Zuhandenheit)*, in which
Dasein considers the possible "for-the-sake-of-which," "toward-which," and "in-order-to" of those utensils. It is this
readiness-to-hand involvement, Heidegger insists, that is Dasein's primordial relationship to other entities. Alternatively,
Dasein may turn its attention from the tool character of objects and see them as "present-at-hand" *(vorhanden)*, the
simple, isolated occurrences of things in space and time.

Perhaps it is easy to criticize Heidegger for idealism in this
account of worldhood. But it would be a misinterpretation to
read this portion of *Being and Time* to imply that the world
suddenly appears only in Dasein's assignment of worldhood to
objects. Heidegger does not mean that a hammer changes per
se in its encounter with Dasein; the intentional *relationship*
fundamentally transforms as Dasein alters its perspective. Dasein's primordial intentionality is manifest in Dasein's ability
to use objects as tools. A hammer is disclosed in space-time as
present-at-hand when abstractly considered as *isolated* in
space-time but disclosed as ready-to-hand when concretely
considered as part of a relational matrix, as an object in-order-
to drive nails for-the-sake-of Dasein. As ready-to-hand, the
hammer is not simply a material object displaying properties
of weight, size, shape, color, and so on but an element of the
worldliness *(Weltlichkeit)* of Dasein's involvements.

Through Dasein's intentional involvements, ready-to-hand
utensils are subject to Dasein's "circumspection" *(Umsicht)*
of the ontical qualities of worldly accommodations in which

Being-in-the-world finds "significance" *(Bedeutsamkeit)*. A pen transfers ink onto paper in the manner I expect, and so it manifests its penhood. However, the significance of the pen lies in its referential character that points to a totality of involvable utensils in which I am implied; the pen is part of a much wider context that includes more than just the ink and the paper, whereby I am led to a comprehension of Being. As William J. Richardson explains, Dasein's

> comprehending of Being always comes-to-pass in and through its comportment with beings, for by Being, after all, is meant simply that by which all things are. [Dasein], then, although comprehending Being *in* itself does not comprehend Being *by* itself, sc. as separate from beings.[3]

As Dasein discovers (or dis-covers, for Heidegger) an instrument, it does so in virtue of an already prediscovered whole composed of interwoven complexes of functional equipment bearing upon each other, which discloses itself as well as the project of the user. This prediscovery of the ready-to-hand is what Heidegger calls Dasein's "concern" *(besorgen),* through which an object refers beyond itself as significance is assigned to it. Heidegger offers evidence that Dasein always has significance in view by explaining what occurs when a utensil's readiness-to-hand is disturbed. For instance, if a hammer is broken or too heavy to use, the hammer becomes "conspicuous." If the hammer is missing, it is said to be "obtrusive." If the hammer is not required for the job but is present and in the way, it is "obstinate." Obtrusive or obstinate, the hammer loses its utensil character and is simply a mass of physical properties: present-at-hand. But if the hammer functions properly, it is *in*-conspicuous, for Dasein's attention is not focused upon the tool but is engaged in the task itself, concerned with the whole involvement, and in-tending to its "environment" *(Umwelt).*

Although Heidegger insists that presence-at-hand is a derivative mode and often couches his discussions in negative language as if presence-at-hand were the "wrong" way to view objects, conspicuousness, obtrusiveness, and obstinacy illustrate the way Being conceals itself. When the in-order-to of the hammer is removed, my circumspection notices a break in the referential fabric in which I was unreflectively involved. But now with the conspicuous hammer in my hand, I realize that the hammer and I were part of that matrix all along. The presence-at-hand of the object draws my view to the hammer's previous mode of readiness-to-hand, and the world is announced. The Being of the whole environment was covered up, even in its referential character. Considering the hammer as present-at-hand cannot alone provide an ontology of Being-in-the-world, but it may illuminate how worldliness is covered up precisely when we are closest to it, that is, when we are not (reflectively) concerned with it.

Heidegger overemphasizes the manipulability of the ready-to-hand and refers to the objects of Dasein's involvements as "equipment" *(das Zeug;* see translators' comments, BT 97 n.1 ). This stress upon the use of tools tends to lead us to think that the world is best disclosed in our exploitation of it. But what Heidegger wishes to illustrate is not Dasein's special ability to manipulate, to work, or to control but the fundamental inhood by which Dasein is involved with and not set apart from the items of its world. It just happens that Heidegger thinks that examples of tool usage best illuminate that involvement. We shall see later that Dasein's solicitude *(Fürsorge)* with other Dasein exhibits another manner of involvement in the world without this emphasis upon use.

When we offer a description of an entity or an account of an event, we speak of the facts of the matter. In giving information about the composition, shape, size, origin, or location of a chair, we relate its "factuality," that which describes the chair as it actually is. Dasein too has its "facts," and what discloses Dasein's *actual* state of existence is its "facticity." *Facticity* does not refer simply to an enumeration of those statements that are true of Dasein, for Heidegger means to point out that Dasein *is* factual in its actual way of existing:

> The concept of "facticity" implies that an entity 'within-the-world' has Being-in-the-world in such a way that it can understand itself as bound up in its 'destiny' with the Being of those entities which it encounters within its own world. . . . *Facticity is not the factuality of the "factum brutum" of something present-at-hand, but a characteristic of Dasein's Being—one which has been taken up into existence, even if proximally it has been thrust aside.* (BT 82, 174)

Although he insists upon the precedence of possibility over actuality, Heidegger emphasizes the influence of the latter upon the former. Dasein exists "there" with given, unalterable factors that condition and limit possible ways of existing. These factual conditions that originally limit possibilities make up Dasein's "thrownness"—those facts primordially given and taken up into the Being of any particular Dasein.

Factical Dasein's actual state of Being as it finds itself "there" in the world is reflected by "states-of-mind" or moods. Heidegger's sense of a state-of-mind is not simply a mental state that reflects an "inner" reaction to an "outer" affair but a lived expression of a concrete state of existing. Heidegger is not concerned here with a psychological account of emotions; he wishes to show that we are always in some mood that reveals the facticity of Being-in-the-world whereby we become aware of our thrownness. (The German term for *mood, Stimmung,* connotes "attunement" with a situation and more fully expresses the intentionality involved in state-of-mind than the English term.) A mood manifests something about my existence that I *have* to be, and the fact *that* I am in such a way of Being in such a situation is brought forth without the origin of the mood itself necessarily being revealed. It is a trusim that we are always in *some* situation, but it should be no less obvious that we are always in *some* mood. We miss the phenomenal sense of moods, Heidegger means to say, if we focus upon psychological or neurophysiological causes or contrast moods with ordinary knowledge claims and beliefs:

> Phenomenally, we would wholly fail to recognize both *what* mood discloses, and *how* it discloses, if that

which is disclosed is to be compared with what Dasein is acquainted with, knows and believes 'at the
same time' when it has such a mood. Even if Dasein is
'assured' in its belief about its 'whither', or . . . its
"whence", all this accounts for nothing as against the
phenomenal facts of the case: for the mood brings Dasein before the "that-it-is" of its "there", which, as
such, stares it in the face with the inexorability of an
enigma. (BT 175)

Instead of being the means by which Dasein attempts to
"figure out" its affairs, moods illustrate the fact that Dasein is
in a particular, actual, concrete way of existing and as such reflect the burdensome character of Being (BT 173). A concrete
depiction of how the burdensome, brutal givenness of the
world is presented to Dasein is shown in the mood of fear.
Something that threatens Dasein may or may not come to pass,
but a fearsome affair has the nature of approaching with a
harmful result—it "means harm." While the fear is in Dasein,
the fear is bound up in the situation in which the approaching
thing and Dasein are each a part, although the *occasion* for the
fear is provided by the upcoming event. The point is that fear
is not merely subjective. For instance, my fear of an upcoming
dental appointment is a characteristic of neither my dentist
nor his office; it is *my* fear in my concern for the situation
*presented* by the visit. I may even be able to ease my fear by reflecting upon previous relatively painless visits. But what is revealed in the fear is that the world so seriously matters to me
that I can be threatened by it. This is not a psychological account of *why* I experience fear. The point is that when I am in
fear, I *am* in a state-of-mind that discloses my facticity as
thrown "there."

As facticity is the existential structure that represents Dasein's actual state of existing, existentiality *(Existenzialität)* is
the structure by which Dasein's possible ways of existing are
disclosed. Also, as facticity is revealed in moods, existentiality
is revealed in "understanding" *(Verstand)*. Further, as state-of-
mind is not meant to refer simply to the contents of psychological states, Heidegger does not mean understanding in the

sense of cognitive activity but the way Dasein exists toward future possibilities so that the future is opened up. In other words, as John Sallis writes, "As Dasein is no subject, so understanding is no immanent representational activity of a subject. Rather, understanding is to be taken up existentially."[4] With understanding as the "sight" of its existentiality, Dasein's disclosure of possibilities is said to have the character of projection *(Entwurf)*. Dis-covering possibilities amounts to Dasein's self-projection "in which it *is* its possibilities as possibilities" (BT 185).

Heidegger speaks of existentiality as the "throwing" of possibilities before Dasein, and Macquarrie and Robinson point out that *Entwurf* and the cognate verb *entwerfen* carry connotations similar to the English verb and noun *project* of not only throwing but also designating a project (BT 185 n. 1). The deep relationship between projection of existentiality and the thrownness of facticity becomes apparent: Dasein is thrown into a world of possibility, and Dasein throws possibility onto its world. To have any possibilities, Dasein must be thrown into a world, but only an entity whose essence lies in its possible ways to exist can be thrown into a world. Heidegger can thus speak of Dasein as "factical potentiality-for-Being" and as having "already projected itself" (BT 185).

### Initial Datum and Subjective Aim

THE SKETCH OF THE HAPPENING of actual occasions in Chapter 2 prepares us for a fuller discussion of the generation of actual occasions. Like Dasein that breaks into its world always already within a network of involvements, the actual occasion's initial act of becoming is an appropriation of the world that reveals the occasion's inhood. The actual occasion does not first exist and then participate in process; to appear in the world is to be originally involved.

Primitive experience lies in the actual occasion's feeling of another actual occasion in its past. Whitehead speaks of the past actual occasion's becoming objectified in the new concrescence as the initial datum of the feeling, but he does not propound an idealist view of feeling the *same* feeling that belonged to the past actual occasion. Although the past actual occasion was its feelings, its subjective immediacy reached satisfaction at its perishing. Objectified as an initial datum, the feeling transferred to the new concrescence is reinterpreted with new immediacy in a novel subjective form belonging only to the becoming of the actual occasion. Insofar as the past actual occasion is felt, there is a direct experience of one event by another, but this experience occurs as a vector. What was there-and-then becomes what is here-and-now. In this way the continuity of the past into the present is preserved, and "the 'power' of one actual entity on the other is simply how the former object is objectified in the constitution of the other" (PR 58).

Whitehead's sense of the universe as an organism is found in the manner the past is reenacted in the present concrescence. The actual occasion cannot be completely novel, for it springs from what has already been. An actual occasion is a unique perspective, but this point of view is a novelty that is relevant to the becoming of continuity. There is, however, no continuity of becoming (PR 35), for actual occasions are the very principles of coherent growth and richness of the universe. Although "the ultimate metaphysical truth is atomism" (PR 35), "each atom is a system of all things" (PR 36). It is the initial act of appropriation of the past that establishes the manner by which the "universe enters into the constitution of the entity in question, so as to constitute the basis of its nascent individuality" (PR 152).

The emergence of the novel actual occasion, however, should not be construed as the singular prehension of one past feeling. Like Dasein in its facticity, the actual occasion is thrown into a multitude of events where "each task of creation is a social effort, employing the whole universe" (PR 223). As Dasein's field of concern lies in the interpretation of its environment, concrescence consists of an interplay of decisions upon what is to be physically felt and what is to be negatively prehended. The diverse (yet coherent) data that make up the actual occasion's world are the conditions of its continuity *and* novelty, and the novel concrescence "finds itself in a web of conditions which convert its exclusions into contrasts" (PR 223). The actual occasion always comes into the world already a potentiality for connection-contrast to its world, for "it belongs to the nature of a 'being' that it is a potential for every 'becoming'" (PR 22). Whitehead calls this notion the principle of relativity, and it expresses his version of the Being-in-the-world of the actual occasion.

However, it is not Heidegger's claim that Dasein's intentional involvement extends to all possible objects, but Whitehead claims that in its objective immortality, the actual occasion is present, in some sense, in every other actual occasion (PR 50). The important point here is that a similar notion of intentionality is at work in both cases. The actual occasion is open to a web of conditions that comprises its facticity, just as Dasein's openness to the world occurs within a matrix of factical relations. Thus, intentionality is already evident in the emergence of the actual occasion by means of the appropriation of an initial datum by an entity that *happens openly* to its world.

The appropriation of an initial datum occurs at once with the ingression of an eternal object that designates the actual occasion's initial aim. The actual occasion is not a bare openness to the world, for concrescence aims at self-creation. Although Whitehead scholars disagree, William A. Christian argues persuasively that the actual occasion's initial aim must be determined by God, for "any selection from among God's feelings by decision of the concrescence would presuppose its initial aim."[5] Within the mental pole of God are prehensions of all potentiality, and God supplies the actual occasion's principle of self-creative aim toward the actualization of one of these potentialities.

But how can the actual occasion be self-creating if its very principle of self-creation is given to it and not selected by it? Donald W. Sherburne says that the "actual occasion has a certain amount of elbow room in its development" by which it modifies "its initial vision of itself."[6] The "originality of the temporal world is conditioned, not determined" (PR 108), by this initial aim, which is vague by virtue of its relation to potential data as not completely determinate. The subjective aim, writes Christian, "grows out of the initial conceptual aim, which has as its datum a possibility not realized in the actual world."[7] As this "basic conceptual feeling suffers simplification in the successive phases of concrescence" (PR 224), the subjective aim becomes more coherent and focused toward the actual occasion's ideal of itself. The activity of projective focusing toward the actual occasion's "significance for itself" (PR 25) in its subjective aim is one way concrescence is fundamentally intentional and represents the actual occasion's existentiality.

Modified in the advance of concrescence, the subjective aim is the "reason of synthesis" by which an actual occasion "defines its own actual world from which it originates" (PR 210). From its own perspective, the self-defining actual occasion interprets the world so that "no two occasions can have identical worlds" (PR 210). For two actual occasions existing simultaneously, it is certainly the case that abstractly, the world is the same for both. But even coexisting occasions occupy (rather, are) unique perspectives on the world; each occasion occurs within its own existential situation. Although these coexisting occasions may prehend the same objective datum, each selects a particular eternal object, in accordance with its subjective aim, as the way the datum is felt. These ways of feeling data "are not merely receptive to the data as alien facts; they clothe the dry bones with the flesh of a real being, emotional, purposive, appreciative" (PR 85). Thus, the self-interpretation of the concrescence is also its interpretation of the world. Whitehead's notion of concrescence as a field for interpretation is practically identical to Heidegger's description of openness. Heidegger claims to lay bare the structures of existence (i.e., to do phenomenology) in the same way that Dasein discloses the world to itself: "Phenomenological Interpretation must make it possible for Dasein itself to disclose things primordially; it must, as it were, let Dasein interpret itself" (BT 179).

Feeling itself in feeling the world, the actual occasion is a *causa sui* (PR 222) that, as F. Bradford Wallack writes, "is not both a subject and an aim."[8] The actual occasion is a subject of experiences that *is* the unifying activity of prehending the world projecting toward self-creation. "There is not an already actual subject which also happens to have an aim; there is not a subject over and above the feelings it has."[9] Whitehead's sense of "subjective" experience must be qualified, for a subject is the growing together, the con-crescence, of feelings that does not imply self-awareness in the ordinary sense. The "subjectivity" of the actual occasion is the activity of "determining its own self-creation as one creature" (PR 69). As mentioned earlier, process is described by two creative movements: the concrescence of the prehending actual occasion and the transition of the satisfied actual occasion as it is appropriated into the constitution of subsequent actual occasions. But given the proper understanding of experiences, we see that these movements are merely two aspects of the same happening. Whitehead expresses the unity of these descriptions in one of his Categories of Explanation: "That *how* an actual entity *becomes* constitutes *what* that actual entity *is;* so that the two descriptions of an actual entity are not independent. Its 'being' is constituted by its 'becoming.' This is the 'principle of process'" (PR 23).

The above passage is remarkably similar to Heidegger's statement that Dasein's essence lies in its existence (BT 67). The way Dasein opens out to the world in its concrete historical situation as finite, ecstatic temporality is what Dasein is; the way the actual occasion interprets its world and passes in to the world as a unique interpretation (i.e., a novel perspective) in temporal process is what the actual occasion is. In this agreement between the two thinkers is their common opposition to substantialist thought. Many philosophers, for example Descartes (PR 151), "presuppose a subject which then encounters a datum, and then reacts to the datum" (PR 155). On the other hand, the thought of both Whitehead and Heidegger "presupposes a datum which is met with feelings, and progressively attains a unity of a subject" (PR 155).[10]

For Whitehead, experience is logically prior to a subject of experiences, for the subject is the projective, coherent growing together of those experiences directed by the subjective aim. Likewise, the experiences of Dasein are pulled together and aimed at death. This nonsubstantialist description of the experiencing subject undercuts the dichotomy of things "out-there" that are represented in the "in here" a containerlike subject. Just as Heidegger writes that experience "is not a process of returning with one's booty to the 'cabinet' of consciousness" (BT 89, quoted earlier), Whitehead bemoans the unfortunate use of such a notion by Locke (PR 54): "The senses at first let in particular ideas, and furnish the yet empty cabinet" (quoted by Whitehead, PR 53 n. 17). The vector nature of prehensions aims what is "there" to "here," but *not* in the sense that something that is there is then *represented* here.

## *Eternal Objects and Subjective Forms*

THE MEDIUM FOR THE vector character of experience, the way what is there is felt here, is an eternal object. Eternal objects are pure potentials. As such, the term *object* is misleading, and Whitehead even says that "if the term 'eternal objects' is disliked, the term 'potentials' would be suitable" (PR 149). Their potentiality lies in their ability to ingress into, that is, become realized in, and contribute to the definiteness of actual occasions. They are said to be pure because they contain in themselves no "necessary reference to any definite actual entities in the temporal world" and are "neutral" to their ingressions (PR 44). They are eternal not in the sense of endlessly enduring but in the sense of being timeless. Examples of eternal objects include sense data (PR 64) or sensa (PR 114), patterns (PR 115), an actual occasion's abstract essence (PR 60), relations within a nexus (PR 194), mathematical concepts (PR 291), and most important for this study, subjective forms considered in abstraction from prehensions (PR 233).

It is a mistake to think of eternal objects as somehow patiently waiting in nonbeing until they are brought into being. Rather, ingression "is the evocation of determination out of indetermination" (PR 149). This determination refers to the eternal object's function as the subjective form of *how* appropriation takes place. When I perceive a red-hot iron, I am not aware, in Whitehead's view, of a substance that has the qualities of heat and redness. The qualia involved in the perspective function adverbially instead of adjectively; that is to say, as Kraus points out, I appropriate "a certain environmental event 'hotly.'"[11] This account is not a description of the composition of the iron rod (which is actually a nexus) but an explanation of my taking over of the rod's feelings in a manner appropriate to my perspectival situation, for the eternal objects ingress into my feeling of the rod and not into the rod.

In contributing to the determination of feelings, eternal objects thereby contribute to the structuring of the concrescence. The full, determinate structure of the actual occasion is the goal of the subjective aim as it proceeds toward satisfaction. In this regard, some aspects of the world will be appropriated as relevant to this aim, and others will be neglected. By the same token, the possibilities presented by eternal objects will be of more or less relevance. Whitehead speaks of the ordering of eternal objects in the actual occasion's subjective aim (PR 43–44). At the same time, eternal objects are subject to a primordial valuation in God. This primordial ordering provides a background of limiting principles of potentiality against which concrescence is set. If eternal objects were presented as a sheer multiplicity, "novelty would be meaningless, and inconceivable" (PR 40). New occasions could never arise without some general, potential coordination of process. God's valuation of pure potentials, then, provides the basis of universal coherence in terms of physical laws that must be obeyed by the concrescence as part of its facticity (PR 283).

As mentioned earlier, even though the actual occasion is composed of feelings of previous feelings from preceding actual occasions, there is no sharing of experiential immediacy. The eternal object makes possible the conformity of the past to the present without events being merely repeated in their objectifications in succeeding actual occasions. Past events are "reenacted" but in relation to a new interpretive purpose found in the subjective aim. This reenactment is due to a double function of the eternal object:

> When there is re-enactment there is one eternal object with a two-way functioning, namely, as partial determinant of the objective datum, and as partial determinant of the subjective form. In this two-way role, the eternal object is functioning relationally between the initial data on the one hand and the concrescent subject on the other. [Yet] It is playing one self-consistent role. (PR 238)

The transition of feelings from one actual occasion to another is better described as reproduction or conformation (PR 238) than as the literal replacing of the same feeling into another occasion. The fact that there are many that can become (not the same) one is explained on Whitehead's view by eternal objects' having different modes of ingression into individuals, so that actual occasions are in part different syntheses of applicable eternal objects. These different modes of ingression are the eternal objects' conformity to the actual occasions' subjective aims.

Ingressing into the actual occasion as the vehicle for interpreting physical feelings in accordance to the subjective aim, the eternal object's role of formulating the subjective form of the feeling belongs to the actual occasion's mental pole. Concretely speaking, though, "this pole is inseparable from the total *res vera*" (PR 70). We recall that facticity and existentiality are not different "parts" of Dasein but abstract ways of speaking about its concrete openness that appropriates and at once projects elements of Dasein's worldly environment. Similarly, the actual occasion does not have a physical part that is then interpreted in a separate operation by its mental part. Just as moods are not merely psychological states but expressions of Dasein's particular situation, subjective forms are the means by which actual occasions express their data from their unique perspectives. Physical feelings enter the actual occasion by means of the same operation that clothes the prehension with the purpose of self-definition. In each prehension, a "reference to the complete actuality is required to give the reason why such a prehension is what is it is in respect to its subjective form" (PR 19). A subjective form may be described as the

intentional character of a prehension's aim toward the wholeness of the actual occasion, for the subjective form "expresses
the purpose which urged [the feeling] forward" (PR 232).

Although the purposive or emotional elements of physical
feelings are due to their subjective forms, they are not bare
experiences of simply given sensations. The perspective of an
actual occasion is more than a receptacle for a sheer multiplicity of sense data; feelings grow together in a perspective. We
should recall that Dasein too has no bare experiences, since it
is always in some mood that reflects Dasein's factical situation
or perspective. Further, since these moods affect experiences
in terms of that situation, we may say that Dasein's experiences
also grow together in a perspective. In this manner, novelty in
process is not found in objectification per se of the content of
feelings but in subjectification of feelings as the subjective
forms pulls them into the unifying activity of concrescence.
Physical feelings are reenactments of past feelings, but not
merely so; they are reenacted in a newly interpreted role from
a novel point of view.

A feeling is the passing from the objectivity of a past actual
occasion to the subjectivity of a concrescencing actual occasion; therefore, feelings always include reference to an external world. Whitehead writes that "the concrescent actuality
arises from feeling [an exterior thing's] status of "individual
particularity'" (PR 55). Thus, although the language Whitehead uses to explain prehension sounds idealistic, actual occasions are not Leibnizian monads feeling only themselves, for
feelings are always feelings "in relevance to a world beyond"
(PR 163). This fundamental intentionality in the vector character of feelings also has the nature of "appetition, which is
the feeling of determinate relevance to a world about to be"
(PR 163). This two-way directionality of physical feelings—
that is, pointing to the actual world whence they arose and to
the world into which the concrescence is becoming—allows
a Whiteheadian translation of the Heraclitean dictum "All
things flow" into "All things are vectors" (PR 309).

This vector character of physical feelings illustrates the
sense in which all actuality is essentially the potentiality to feel

and to be felt. This leads to a consideration of the "second stage" of concrescence, conceptual feelings. While the data of physical feelings, abstractly considered, are the past actual occasions of the feelings' origins, the data of conceptual feelings are the eternal objects attached to those prehensions. With each physical prehension, the eternal object involved in the subjective form of the feeling is conceptually felt in "its *capacity* for being a realized determinant of process" (PR 239). The eternal object is immanent in the actual occasion insofar as it ingresses as a subjective form, but its transcendence of any particular determination in particular concrescences is conceptually felt as pure potentiality. In this way a conceptual feeling is the grasping of an eternal object as an element contributing to the structuring of concrescence. The many feelings involved in the actual occasion are "transformed into a unity of aesthetic appreciation," that is, appetition (PR 212). The actual occasion's deal of itself at which it aims in satisfaction is related to its vision of a potential world into which the actual occasion may pass.

The actual occasion's conceptual appetition toward a potential world arises by means of "hybrid physical feelings" leading to "conceptual reversion." All possibilities relevant (and irrelevant) to a concrescence are contained in God. God prehends relationships among eternal objects that limit their ingressions. There is, however, a range of indeterminacy that presents alternatives to the concrescing actual occasion. In a hybrid physical feeling, the actual occasion conceptually prehends the alternatives relevant to its subjective aim as conditioned also by the limits presented by preceding actual occasions. While ordinary conceptual feelings derive from physical feelings of past actual occasions, reverted conceptual feelings derive from the present actual occasion's hybrid physical feelings of God.[12] At the same time, conceptually reverted feelings are related to simple physical feelings in that their data "are partially identical with, and partially diverse from, the eternal objects forming the data" of ordinary conceptual feelings (PR 249). This means that the eternal objects prehended in a reverted conceptual feeling are the same as some of those that have already ingressed into the actual occasion in previous physical feelings as subjective forms, but novelty is introduced as these eternal objects are prehended *in* this potentiality.

I have presented only a rough sketch of a highly technical description of a particular sort of prehension. Such complicated descriptions abound in *Process and Reality,* and they are often more opaque than clear or consistent. Nevertheless, the category of conceptual reversion is intended to illustrate how genuine novelty, which is always in conformity to the internal coherence of concrescence and the external harmony of transition, can arise in conceptual feelings in spite of the fact that "Hume's principle of the derivation of conceptual experience from physical experience remains without any exception" (PR 250).[13] A strict empiricist epistemology is certainly implied in that statement, but Whitehead's treatment of the objects of sensation certainly differs from that of his empiricist predecessors.

Since a sensum is a function of the ingression of an actual occasion, it can be considered neither a particular nor a universal in the old senses. Insofar as the realization of a sensum "does not involve the concurrent realization of certain definite eternal objects," it is simple; yet a sensum is in another sense complex, "for it cannot be dissociated form its potentiality for ingression into *any* actual entity" (PR 114). More importantly, Locke, typifying previous empiricists, "assumes that the utmost primitiveness is to be found in sense-perception" (PR 113). For Whitehead, something deeper is at work in immediated experience, for "more primitive types of experience are concerned with sense-reception, and not with sense-perception" (PR 113). What are received in these sense receptions as sensa "are emotional forms transmitted from occasion to occasion" (PR 114).

The emotional content of feelings is due to the concern that actual occasions have for the world, for "it belongs to the essence of each occasion of experience that it is concerned with an otherness."[14] But the otherness about which the actual occasion is concerned is not foreign and distant but intimate. It should be clear by now that for Whitehead, as Kraus writes, it is not the case that

the perceiver [is] external to the perceived, as a privi-
ledged observer uninvolved in the system observed.
Nature for the perceiver is a total relational event of
which the perceiver is a part. A perceptive event is
situated "here" and "now" within nature and is bound
to the relativity of a perspective. . . . In this context,
to perceive an event is to grasp or become aware of the
natural relations of the perceiving event to the rest of
nature.[15]

Situated within nature, the actual occasion "has a perfectly
definite bond with each item in the universe" by which they
"form a system, in the sense of entering into each other's constitution" (PR 41).

Dasein's care makes possible its experience of the world as
involved relations in a matrix of possibilities. Even those items
Dasein is not directly involved with have their "places" in the
matrix of Dasein's environment. Heidegger does not claim that
Dasein's experience is characterized by a concern for *every*
item in the universe. Even so, the referential nature of this
system of involvements opens out so that the world *is* the
potentiality of Dasein's involvements. But since Dasein is a
spatiotemporally finite field of openness, its involvements
cannot actually extend to all things. Yet we could say that Dasein is *potentially* involved with any item in the universe,
though *actually* involved with only some. Perhaps this notion
is not so far from Whitehead's theory of negative prehensions
by which the actual occasion is related to all other actual occasions. While the actual physical content of the actual occasion is composed of positive feelings, the actual occasion is
potentially related to those items that it excludes from its positive content. Whitehead even says that "each negative prehension has its own subjective form, however trivial and faint,"
and "adds to the emotional complex, though not to the objective data" (PR 41).

Given its concrete situation, that is, its unique perspective
with an aim toward a novel wholeness, the actual occasion
positively experiences certain items as part of its constitution
while yet being potentially defined by its negative prehensions.

Given its concrete historical situation—that is, its unique spatio-temporal and factical placing within its environment—Dasein directly experiences certain items through its circumspective concern while yet being open toward a larger world that includes and refers to items not directly experienced. In this manner both Whitehead and Heidegger conceive of the world as a system of events engaged in a process of interrelatedness made possible by the ontological openness essential to experience. However, this openness is always limited by the experiencer's perspective, but this situation is experienced *as* being exceeded by the world. The next step, then, is to reveal how Whitehead's and Heidegger's transcendental approach shows how our experience is possible through our finitude.

# 4

# *The How of Finitude*

WHAT THE ACTUAL OCCASION and Dasein are can be understood in discovering how they experience the world. How they experience the world can be understood in discovering how they exist. Although the actual occasion and Dasein enjoy an infinite range of possible experience, they exist as temporally finite, and the way they experience is fundamentally affected by their finitude. We remember that for Kant, the great originator of the transcendental method, to ground our experience is necessarily to limit it: only by knowing the limited applications of concepts do we understand the necessary structures of experience and thus the structures of the experienceable world. While I have noted that Whitehead's and Heidegger's approaches differ importantly from that of Kant, they share the view that we understand the possibility of experience only in understanding it to be finite.

## *The "Who" of Dasein*

HEIDEGGER'S HERMENEUTIC EXEGESIS of Dasein's lived experience reveals much about the Being of encountered things. But exactly what or who is this entity that encounters? Heidegger's answer lies in explicating an obvious but often forgotten (in traditional ontology) truth: Dasein is not alone in the world.

Fundamentally, Dasein exists as Being-with-Others, and "its understanding of Being already implies the understanding of others" (BT 161). Heidegger does not mean a gregariousness resulting from social conditioning but that

> Dasein 'is' essentially for the sake of Others. This must be understood as an existential statement as to its essence. Even if the particular factical Dasein does *not* turn to Others, and supposes that it has no need of them or manages to get along without them, it *is* in the manner of Being-with *[Mitsein]*. (BT 160)

In the same manner that Heidegger shows that in Dasein's experience of the world of things "a bare subject without a world never 'is' proximally, . . . so in the end an isolated 'I' without Others is just as far from being proximally given" (BT 152). Always already involved with Others, Dasein exhibits "solicitude" *(Fürsorge)* and finds itself in a *Mitwelt* characterized by "everydayness," that is, "a definite 'how' of existence by which Dasein is dominated through and through 'for life'" (BT 422). Even Dasein's circumspective concern for the ready-to-hand includes recognition of the involvements of Others in the relational matrix of Dasein's environment (BT 153–54).

Domination by everydayness tends to cover up Dasein's self. Others encountered by Dasein in solicitous involvements are "those for whom, for the most part, one does *not* distinguish oneself" (BT 154). Yet in considering who it is, Dasein characterizes itself by *"what* it does, uses, expects, avoids—in those things environmentally ready-to-hand with which it is proximally *concerned"* (BT 155). This apparent conflict in Dasein's identifying itself with worldly activities is resolved by recognizing that Others can assume those activities. Someone else can utilize the equipment in my environment and even take over my plans. In this sense, Dasein is interchangeable with Others. Such everyday replaceability locates Dasein within "the they" in which "everyone is the other, and no one is himself" (BT 165). Macquarrie and Robinson use "the they" for Heidegger's *"das Man,"* a term that suggests that Dasein is within the crowd and carries less implication of separateness than the English term. Further, Heidegger's use of the neuter article tends to make the term more thinglike than personal.

Heidegger says that everydayness has the characteristic of "averageness" in which Dasein's projects become role-playing by following prescribed norms. Caught up in fads and standards, Dasein's discourse is reduced to "idle talk" in which the public way of interpreting things is given to Dasein, so that a penetrating understanding of Being is closed off. Schrag explains that

> what comes to expression is the flattened, shallow, conventionalized mode of the anonymous and impersonal one *(Das Man).* . . . The originative and creative character of the word as spoken is threatened and speech degenerates into a morass of cliches and superficial observations. What is at issue is no longer the fecund word which is created each time that it is uttered, but rather the sterile locution of a flattened existence.[1]

Unlike the logos that lets something be seen, idle talk dictates an attitude for observing the world. Forgetting that language should allow entities to "be appropriated in a primordial manner" (BT 212), Dasein believes certain things to be the case because "they" say so, and gossip and rumor replace truth.

Instead of reflecting Dasein's openness to Bring, the language of idle talk covers up, and Dasein views the world in "curiosity" in which the purpose is not to understand but simply to observe. Curiously glancing from one object to another, Dasein's circumspection becomes a series of distractions without taking time to allow for concernful grasping of meaning. By *"not tarrying alongside what is closest"* (BT 216), Dasein has the feature of *"never dwelling anywhere [Aufentholtslosigkeit]"* (BT 217). Carelessly chattering about curious distractions, Dasein's understanding is "ambiguous," closed off to the point that anything, hence nothing, can be said of anything, and the world is covered up and passed by.

These features of average everydayness exemplify the way

Dasein's finite possibilities of existence are leveled down and further limited. The they limits and forces possibilities upon Dasein so that they are not freely chosen at all; thus, "the particular Dasein in its everydayness is *disburdened* by the 'they'" (BT 165): the responsibility of choosing ways to exist is relieved by the anonymity of averageness. What is most important here is Heidegger's insistence that an irresistible *"downward plunge [Absturz]"* (BT 223) into everydayness is unavoidable, for "fallenness," along with finitude and existentiality, is the third existential structure of care. Continually falling into and being absorbed by the they, Dasein welcomes the "tranquility" of the they's assurance of the safest, "best" order of things. But the consequence of this security is that Dasein forfeits its "mineness" to the they. We should keep in mind, however, that Heidegger does not mean that Dasein loses something like an ego-self to become a pathetic, unoriginal creature; what Dasein stands to lose is its potentiality for Being.

In spite of stating that "falling reveals an *essential* ontological structure of Dasein itself" (BT 224), Heidegger says that Dasein can rescue its mineness to achieve "authenticity." (It is important to note that the term Macquarrie and Robinson translate is *"eigentlich,"* and the term for *own* is *eigen.*) To understand this, we must see how care *(Sorge)* is the Being of Dasein and how its three structures of existentiality, facticity, and fallenness are unified in temporal horizons.

### *Anxiety and Death*

DASIEN IS A FIELD OF intentional openness that makes possible its involvements with equipment and Others. But this very openness that makes Dasein what it is leads to an absorption in the world, so that falling Dasein's mineness becomes scattered amid involvements with Others in average everydayness. The possibility of Dasein's authentic unity is ignored, and sight is turned away from the meaning of Dasein's Being. Since this inauthentic way of existing is Dasein's ordinary, actual state of Being, this situation must be revealed in a mood. Heidegger tells us that the particular mood in this case is anxiety *(Angst)*, and anxiety draws attention to Dasein's finite, ecstatic temporality that is the meaning of care. As the actual occasion focuses and projects itself toward self-definition in its subjective aim, Dasein recognizes through anxiety that its forfeited and scattered mineness can be recovered and focused in its aim toward death.

Anxious Dasein is for a moment freed from the security of everydayness and feels "uncanny" *(unheimlich)*, or not at home in the world. The comfort of busying itself in the ambiguous distractions of the they seem out of Dasein's reach as the world of the familiar fades. A surrounding emptiness takes hold of Dasein as its involvements appear insignificant. While fear occurs in the presence of some object in the world, and we always experience fear as fear of some *thing*, anxiety is objectless, for it stands in the face of Being-in-the-world itself. Dasein encounters the "nothing" behind its average comportment with the world, the groundlessness of Dasein's everydayness that causes Dasein to wish to return to the tranquility of the they. Just as a conspicuous tool becomes present-at-hand and serves to light up the worldhood of the ready-to-hand, the emptiness of everydayness felt in anxiety presents to Dasein the full force of its Being.

Faced with the tremendous responsibility of achieving a ground for itself, Dasein asks what might be lost in returning to the security of the they. Heidegger's answer is "nothing"; but the loss of this nothing is Dasein's loss of itself. It is the disclosure of its groundlessness of itself in everydayness that provides the opportunity for authentic existence. In anxiety "there lies the possibility of a disclosure which is quite distinctive; for anxiety individualizes. This individualization brings Dasein back from its falling and makes manifest to it that authenticity and inauthenticity are possibilities of its Being" (BT 225).

Anxiety reveals the structural whole of care and hints at the meaning of care as temporality. As state-of-mind, anxiety is a way for Dasein to exist, and it reveals that "in the face of which we have anxiety is Being-in-the-world" (BT 235). Anxiety also underlines the fact that Dasein is an entity for which Being is an issue, for "that which we have anxiety about is potentiality-for-Being-in-the-world" (BT 235). This potentiality is what constitutes existentiality; anxiety in the face of thrownness into Being-in-the-world reflects facticity; and finally, fallenness is disclosed by Dasein's feeling of uncanniness as average everydayness is brought to light. Heidegger expresses the unity of care evident in anxiety in this schema: "ahead-of-itself-Being-already-in (the world) as being-alongside entities we encounter (within the world)" (BT 293). In this schema are included the three "fundamental characteristics of Dasein's Being: existence [existentiality], in the 'ahead of itself'; facticity, in the 'Being-already-in'; falling, in the 'Being-alongside'" (BT 293).

This schema already points to Dasein's temporality: "ahead of itself" implies Dasein's futural character; "Being-already-in" contains Dasein's past; and the present is indicated in "Being-alongside." In the explication of this schema, we clearly see Heidegger's transcendental inquiry explicitly at work. To speak of temporality as the *meaning* of care is to speak of temporality as that which constitutes or makes care possible. The meaning of anything for Heidegger is not given by a definition but concerns the possibilities of what is in question. Existentiality is the futural component of this meaning in regard to Dasein's openness to potential ways to be. We are always ahead of ourselves in that we are not restricted to a present way of existing in the manner that what is present-at-hand is. This ecstatic, temporal transcendence is also found in the manner that we have always already taken up past possibilities. These past possibilities are not over and done with; rather, they ever exemplify *how* we are always thrown into Being-in-the-world. Finally, Dasein's present state of fallenness is disclosed in anxiety as existing alongside that to which Dasein forfeits its mineness and removed from which Dasein feels uncanny— that is, the they.

Heidegger explains that the temporality of anxiety is central to the possibility of authenticity: "Anxiety is grounded in having been, and only out of this do the future and Present temporalize themselves; in this peculiar temporality is demonstrated the possibility which is distinctive for the mood of anxiety" (BT 394). Given Heidegger's emphasis on the horizon of the future, anxiety's grounding in the past makes its temporality peculiar. This primordial grounding allows for the transparency of Dasein's thrownness. Anxious Dasein, as opposed to what is characteristic of average everydayness, does not view itself in terms of what is presently curious, ambiguous, and the subject of idle talk. Anxiety calls up the bare that-it-is of thrown Dasein that in its inauthenticity has become the property of the they. But in uncanniness, Dasein looks beyond its present state to the responsibility of projecting from its thrownness upon its possibility to be its own. In so doing, Dasein may uncover what it authentically is and free itself from the anonymity of the they.

Heidegger maintains that Dasein's possibility to regain itself from the inauthentic existence of levelled-down possibilities and self-alienation is not an impulsive act, for Dasein is "summoned" to authenticity by the call of "conscience" *(Gewissen),* a call that "comes *from* me and yet *from beyond me and over me*" (BT 320). Ultimately, the call is Dasein calling itself, but the voice sounds alien and distant, for it is from Dasein's potential authenticity as heard in inauthenticity. Dispersed within the they, Dasein cannot recognize its own innermost voice, and the deeper it has fallen into everydayness, the more likely it is to misinterpret the call. If Dasein harkens to the call, it stands face-to-face with only itself and hears the call in the form of a charge: Guilty! Dasein is guilty of a debt not to others but to itself. Dasein may pay this debt by giving back to itself what it lacks in its Being. (The term Heidegger uses for *guilt* is *"Schuld,"* meaning "lack.") In recognizing this nullity, Dasein sees that it "is something that has been thrown; it has been brought into its 'there', but *not* of its own accord" (BT 329). Although Dasein did not cause itself, Heidegger maintains that in the end, only Dasein is responsible for its Being; thus, thrownness, which is at the basis of Dasein's Being, must be "delivered over, and as such [Dasein] can exist solely as the entity which it is" (BT 330).

Guilty Dasein has failed to take up its thrownness and as such failed at Being-one's-Self *(Selbstsein).* The guilt of this failure is not like the guilt we experience when we commit an immoral act, for "Dasein is essentially guilty—not just *on some occasions,* and on *other occasions not*" (BT 353). Because Dasein exists as fallen, it continually covers up its mineness: *"Care itself, in its very essence, is permeated with nullity through and through"* (BT 331). To be authentic, Dasein must continually heed the call of conscience by wanting to have a conscience; that is, Dasein must want to be reminded of its fallenness and must want to engage in a dialogue with the caller. This dialogue between the caller and the receiver who accepts its anxious attunement to Being-in-the-world takes place in keeping silent *(Schweigen).* This silence is contrasted with everydayness in that it "takes the words away from the commonsense idle talk of the 'they'" (BT 343).

The three ways of Dasein's disclosure are revealed in this dialogue: (1) Understanding: Dasein understands itself as guilty and projects possibilities on the basis of the nullity of its thrownness. (2) State-of-mind: In the uncanniness of anxiety, Dasein recognizes that its thrownness has been forfeited to the they, and yet this very uncanniness individualizes Dasein from the they. (3) Discourse: The silence of the call and the reticence of the response indicates that Dasein needs no instruction about its authenticity. Although fallenness is the third component of care, it is not a part of Dasein's disclosure, for fallenness is what leads to the continual covering up of Dasein's mineness. As logos, discourse has its purpose in revealing Being. Gadamer writes:

> Language is not just one of man's possessions in the world, but on it depends the fact that man has a world at all. . . . To have a 'world' means to have an attitude towards it. To have an attitude towards the world, however, means to keep oneself so free from what one encounters of the world that one is able to present it to oneself as it is. This capacity is both the having of a 'world' and the having of language.[2]

The authentic discourse of conscience reveals that Dasein's world, which includes Dasein's (fragmented) self, has been taken over and covered up by the they. But by accepting its guilt and undertaking to dis-cover itself through its discourse with conscience, Dasein can come to "resoluteness," the *reticent self-projection upon one's ownmost Being-guilty, in which one is ready for anxiety"* (BT 343). Heidegger uses the term *Entschlossenheit,"* from the verb *schliessen,* "to lock." So resolute Dasein unlocks itself from the restrictions of the they. Further, we should note the etymological connection between the terms *Entschlossenheit* and *Erschlossenheit,* "disclosedness" (BT 343 n. 1). Although resoluteness refers primarily to reappropriating one's thrownness and is therefore basically grounded in having been (i.e., the authentic past as opposed to what is inauthentically seen as merely past and gone), there is also a futural character to resoluteness, for *"it harbours in itself authentic Being-towards-death, as the possible existentiell modality of its own authenticity"* (BT 353). Resolute projection must be considered along with Dasein's anticipation of its own death. The intentionality of Dasein's toward-the-end will show how Dasein, as Joseph P. Fell writes, "is free to surrender to the temporal ground as the clearing within which Dasein is possible at all."[3]

Heidegger's discussion of "death" involves neither the physiological events that make up the process of dying nor its psychological features. Nor is Heidegger concerned with the possibility of an afterlife, for if there is any state of being beyond death, it must occur apart from Dasein's Being-in-the-world and thus is not Dasein. Heidegger is interested in the existential phenomenon of being that must, and knows it must, someday not be, a being that is forced to view its existence as finite, a being that must either hide from the fact that it moves toward its own end or accept this fact as part of its facticity.

Our everyday attitude toward death is an exercise in convincing ourselves that death is far away and of no consequence now. As fallen, we cover up death in the same ways we cover up the Being of other things: idle talk says that death will come "when my time comes"; it is always "them, not me," who die, and since I "cannot do anything about it," any discussion serves only to produce morbid feelings. We are, however, curious about the deaths of others and wish to find out all the fascinating details of another's demise. Subjected to the ambiguity of this attitude, death is given an interpretation that gives me the reassurance that death is something that happens, but not to me. Heidegger insists that this "flight from death" leads us to think that we have infinite time to continue with our everyday affairs.

The authentic view, however, forces upon me the realization that although the particular occasion of my death is indefinite, the fact *that* I must die is certain. I realize that my potentiality-for-Being will come to a close, and although my authentic concern is not for my *actual* death, I understand death to be a possibility that is my "ownmost." Anxiously before myself and without the support of the they, I see that my death cannot be shared by or transferred to others; death is "nonrelational." Even though another may sacrifice his life for mine in some particular event, no one can remedy my death as an ontological condition. For in spite of the fact that my death may be delayed, it is always certain that I must die. Thus, although anxiety is grounded primarily in facticity and death must be resolutely accepted as a "fact" of Dasein, this acceptance reveals existentiality in Dasein's existence *toward* death as its ownmost, individuating possibility.

While existing, Dasein is always incomplete. "There is constantly *something still to be settled* . . . something still outstanding in one's potentiality-for-Being" (BT 279). But at death Dasein ceases to be, and this perishing provides a temporal end by which we can begin to see Dasein as a whole.

However, a paradox now arises, for the "possibility of Being-a-whole is manifestly inconsistent with the ontological meaning of care . . . [, for] the primary item in care is the 'ahead of itself'" (BT 279). The question is If Dasein is primarily futural, how is it that its ownmost possibility is one that eradicates the future? This paradox fades when it is shown that death is not simply the last in a series of events but is the completion of Dasein. Authentic Dasein does not consider death the point where possibilities simply run out but a phenomenon that serves as the background upon which all other possibilities are projected. James M. Demske writes that Dasein's possibilities

> can only be authentically understood and brought to realization if they are seen in the light and perspective of the preeminent possibility of death. The unity of Dasein . . . requires that all of its retrievable, repeatable, intermediate, and thus secondary possibilities be built into the primary, unrepeatable, and irretrievable possibility of death.[4]

Authentic Dasein exists *toward* the ultimate possibility of its futurity and aims at death as the concretion of its finitude. Using death as the projective background, Dasein is said to exist in "anticipation" *(Vorlaufen)* of death.

In the anticipation of Being-toward-death, accepting death as one's own implies understanding what one really is. This understanding entails an acceptance of one's irreversible thrownness that includes the unsurpassable possibility of death, the possibility that carries with it all previous possibilities, so that Dasein, as Alfonso Lingis states it, "forms the unity of one death-bound trajectory."[5] Heidegger writes that since

> anticipation of the possibility which is not to be outstripped discloses all the possibilities which lie ahead of that possibility, this anticipation includes the possibility of taking the *whole* of Dasein in advance *[Vorwegnehmens]* in an existentiell manner; that is to say, it includes the possibility of existing as a *whole potentiality-for-Being.* (BT 309)

As anticipation becomes the determining attitude for authentic Dasein's concern for the world and solicitude for Others, Dasein's projections include the whole of its Being; thrownness, guilt, and resoluteness are included, for authentic Dasein must anticipate *resolutely.* Choosing resolutely, I choose to do so (at least try to) as long as I exist—that is, until my death.

The union of anticipation and resoluteness occur existentielly, for anticipatory resoluteness is a way that may or may not occur in ontic situations. Michael E. Zimmerman comments that although anticipation is "an existential-ontological possibility requiring verification," resoluteness is "the existentiell-ontical verification that anticipation of one's death is possible. Authentic existence is resolute anticipation of one's own death."[6]

While anticipatory resoluteness is the phenomenological schema for authenticity, we have not yet clearly seen how this way of existing temporally unifies Dasein. Heidegger calls this unity *"constancy of the Self, . . .* the *authentic* counter-possibility to the non-Self-constancy which is characteristic of irresolute falling" (BT 369). The task is to show how the process of events in which Dasein is unified from birth, which is no more, to death, which is not yet. We shall see in the next chapter that the analysis of this "betweenness," or Dasein's "happening" *(Geschehen),* amounts to a discussion of Dasein's ecstatic "historicality." Furthermore, while historicality provides the key to understanding authenticity as the awareness and appropriation of one's finite, ecstatic temporality, Dasein's "ends" of birth and death reveal horizontal features by which Dasein, in a sense, extends beyond its own concrete boundaries.

## Consciousness

WE HAVE JUST SEEN that we discover who Dasein is by revealing how it exists in everydayness. Fallenness levels possibilities, and Dasein is engulfed in the they. An even more powerful illustration of Dasein's finitude is found in the anxious awareness of certain death. Yet the very awareness of this finitude makes possible Dasein's authentic how of existence. For Whitehead too, the recognition that our relations in the world are always finite is precisely what discloses the possibility of these relations. This sort of recognition is characteristic of our conscious experience.

Consciousness, according to Whitehead, is not itself a prehension but the subjective form of "intellectual" feelings. These feelings are enjoyed by only some actual occasions, and such feelings have as their data a contrast between a nexus and a proposition. The propositions involved in these feelings are the expressions of "certain actual entities in their potentiality for forming a nexus," with those actual entities as the "logical subjects" and the eternal object (that potentiality) as the "predicate" (PR 24). Propositions, then, are not facts about the world in the way that actual occasions are, for propositions are ways that collections of actual occasions *might* be felt to be in certain relationships. Yet neither are they pure potentials in the way eternal objects are, for propositions refer to definite things.

Consciousness is the way the degree of conformity between the nexus and the proposition is felt, and thereby consciousness always contains "reference to definiteness, affirmation, and negation" (PR 243). Concerned with the affirmation-negation contrast presented by the intellectual application of the proposition to the actual occasion's feeling of the nexus, consciousness can be said to be "the feeling of what is relevant to immediate fact in contrast with its potential irrelevance" (PR 268).

To propose that X could be Y but in fact is not, is the basis of consciousness. Consciousness for Whitehead is not a separate activity occurring apart from or parallel to other forms of feeling. All actual occasions enjoy conceptual feelings, but consciousness is a higher form of "mental" activity that is dependent upon the lower forms. To affirm that the stone is gray is to have a physical feeling of a nexus of a more primitive sort. To entertain the possibility that the stone is not gray is the advent of the higher form that is consciousness, for the "negative perception is the triumph of consciousness" (PR 161). Since all experiences are elements in the self-creative development of actual occasions, the higher sorts of feelings whose subjective forms are consciousness are "the intellectual self-analysis of the entity in an earlier stage of incompletion" (PR 56).

The actual occasion has already prehended the nexus in a transmuted physical feeling by experiencing this collection of actual occasions by means of an eternal object that expresses a relationship among those occasions. Thus, this collection of occasions is felt as if it were one entity. The actual occasion may then take this datum and conceptually vary it to include possible interpretations of what its world *might have been* like. In doing so, the actual occasion entertains possible ways it might be in concrescence as opposed to the way it actually, finitely exists in concrescence. So consciousness is the subjective form of feeling "the contrast between *'in fact'* and *'might be,'* in respect to particular instances in *this* actual world" (PR 267). The actual occasion has an awareness of the potentiality of process in its feeling of what could be but is absent, "and it feels this absence as produced by the definiteness exclusive of what is really present" (PR 273).

Whitehead, then, does not characterize consciousness as a grasping of what is; rather, consciousness is concerned with what is not. But the events are "not," not because of some impossibility but because they are possible yet unactualized. They are possibilities that could have been in the concrescence of the actual occasion, but the actual occasion cannot be everything. Heidegger writes that an entity essentially characterized by its potentiality "always stands in one possibility or another; it constantly is *not* other possibilities, and it has waived these in its existentiell projection" (BT 331). Any entity whose existential constitution is fundamentally in the temporal process exists as futural projection, and *"as projection* it is itself essentially *null"* (BT 331). By relating itself to some other entities negatively, only by closing off possibilities of projection through negative prehensions, the freedom in the temporal advance of concrescence is established. As Heidegger says, "Freedom, however, *is* only in the choice of one possibility—that is, in tolerating one's not having chosen the others and one's not being able to choose them" (BT 331). This freedom in the recognition of what is chosen, in the contrast between what is and what is not (but could have been), is most illuminated in the conscious way of experiencing.

Heidegger does not claim that Dasein is not conscious of its involvements. It would be patently false to maintain that the carpenter is never aware of swinging the hammer and striking the nail. Rather, Heidegger's message is that conscious experience is not what makes the carpenter's involvement with his equipment possible. Prior to any conscious experience, the carpenter exists as the kind of entity that is open to the possibility of hammer involvements (primarily because he has hammer-accommodating hands), of which he may be more or less conscious. Neither does Heidegger merely emphasize the fact that we often become so engrossed in an activity that our behavior is second nature. We all become wrapped up in tasks that seem to require little thought and hardly remember doing afterward. Heidegger's claim is more profound: Dasein is primarily a field for involvements to happen and secondarily a creature that thinks about those involvements.

Furthermore, it seems that authenticity must be understood in terms of a conscious act of resoluteness. Dasein comes to understand itself as average, everyday existence and sees that it may exist in another way. However, it is not this conscious act that interests Heidegger but the underlying structure of ecstatic temporality (which is not an ingredient in consciousness but something about which Dasein may be aware) that makes possible any of Dasein's ways of existing. Dasein may exist as absorbed into and scattered amid its involvements with the ready-to-hand and with Others, or Dasein may grasp that which makes its involvements possible so that it may call those involvements "mine."

For Whitehead too, the actual occasion is primarily an entity that is involved in the world by its physical prehensions and secondarily (for some) an entity that enjoys conscious experiences about those prehensions. As Dasein's involvements with the ready-to-hand and Others are made possible by structures that form its openness, so are the actual occasion's experience of physical feelings made possible by its openness to past actual occasions. In both cases, consciousness depends upon these prior processes. Again we see Whitehead's and Heidegger's transcendental inquiries at work, for it is the openness to the world that explains our intentional involvement with the world, which in turn explains the possibility of consciousness.

## Satisfaction and Objective Immortality

As DASEIN VIEWS DEATH to be the aim of the concretion of its futurity, the toward-which of the actual occasion's subjective aim is its satisfaction, "one complex, fully determinate feeling" (PR 26). The datum of this final feeling is a concrete unity of all its previous positive and negative feelings of other actual occasions, eternal objects, and propositions. The occasion's prehension of all elements of the universe are brought together, and unlike any antecedent stage in concrescence, satisfaction eliminates all indeterminations concerning its possible responses to the given world. As Christian points out, the satisfaction is the final outcome of concrescence, but it cannot be understood apart from concrescence, for "satisfaction embodies the history of its own becoming."[7] The attainment of satisfaction "closes up the entity" (PR 84), so that its "subjective" concern is complete and it becomes a "superject," a term that Whitehead prefers over the dulaism-implying *object*. As well as embodying its history, the superjective satisfaction "embodies what the entity is beyond itself" (PR 219) by adding itself to the given world of successive actual occasions.

With satisfaction, the actual occasion is said to perish.[8] Indeed, Whitehead says that process is characterized by perpetual perishing (PR 81–82), and we are reminded that Heidegger says that Dasein is always dying. Only as finite can Dasein unify itself in its aim toward death, and the actual occasion must achieve satisfaction and perish if it is to pull all its prehensions together into a final feeling. Just as death is the point at which all possibilities run out, although Dasein remains as a field of possibility for future Dasein, the actual occasion becomes a determinate, unchanging actuality to be interpreted by future actual occasions. However, the status of the actual occasion changes, for its perishing marks it as a superject in transition. In *Science and Philosophy,* Whitehead says that perishing "is the one key thought around which the whole development of *Process and Reality* is woven."[9] For Heidegger, Dasein's repetition of past possibility ensures that the past is not merely a string of dead actualities beyond reach. For Whitehead, the very fact that the actual occasion is temporally finite and perishes provides the way the past is not lost, for without perishing, writes David R. Mason, process "might be construed as a sheer, characterless flow, a continuous becoming, rather than as a creative advance."[10]

Whitehead's treatment of perishing is not described in the highly emotional terms of Heidegger's elaboration upon guilt-ridden anxiety before death. Yet it is clear that for both thinkers, the finitude of entities is crucial to their becoming. Whitehead writes, "How the past perishes is how the future becomes,"[11] for the perished actual occasion, though no longer becoming, is cast forth into transition. As the possibilities of Dasein-that-has-been are forever open to retrieval by succeeding Dasein, the perished actual occasion achieves "objective immortality" by forever remaining an element, either positively or negatively prehended, in the concrescence of future actual occasions. As well as anticipating its own end in its subjective aim, the actual occasion anticipates the future that lies beyond its perishing:

> For it is inherent in the constitution of the immediate, present actuality that a future will supersede it. Also conditions to which that future must conform, including real relationships to the present, are really objective in the immediate actuality. . . . [The actual occasion] really experiences a future which must be actual, although the completed actualities of the future are undermined. In this sense, each actual occasion experiences its own objective immortality. (PR 215)

The intentionality of the subjective aim toward its satisfaction includes anticipatory feelings of an intentional appetition toward its transcendent future; in this sense, the actual occasion transcends itself.

The becoming of the actual occasion, then, includes both its concrescence and its transition: it is at once subject and superject (PR 29, 45). Insofar as the unity of the actual occasion's feelings is undetermined, it is a subject; insofar as these feelings are unified into definiteness, it is a superject. In addition to the dipolarity of an actual occasion's physical and mental sides, the subject's directing its feelings toward itself as superject manifests the dipolar rhythm of process: "It swings from the publicity of many things to the individual privacy; and it swings back from the private individual to the publicity of the objectified individual" (PR 151). This public-private dipolarity, by which no thing is completely a subject or completely an object, renders a distinction between internal and external relations impossible. The real, internal constitution of an actual occasion is composed of its external relations, and external relations are real only in becoming constituents of the prehending concrescence. Here we have the Being-in-the-world of the actual occasion, always already presupposing its world of relations and never outside those relations.

Always subject-superject, the actual occasion reveals its finite, ecstatic temporality. Open to its factical heritage, it inherits its possibilities from the past. But what is inherited is always appropriated as futurally projected in its subjective aim toward satisfaction. Projecting itself toward its concrete, temporal perishing, the actual occasion feels itself *as* moving toward its end in its vision of itself as objectively immortal. The potentiality of the future is just as immanent in the concrescence as is the past. "The aim of feelings at a subject-superject," writes Wallack, "is their aim at a present concrescence and a future possibility," and the future is thus "the reconstructed past."[12] For both Heidegger and Whitehead, the primacy of the future is what gives meaning to temporality, because, writes Whitehead, if we "cut away the future, . . . the past collapses, emptied of its proper content."[13]

This chapter has cleared the way for a deeper understanding of how ecstatic temporality allows essentially historical Dasein to retrieve possibilities from the past and to have an understanding of time itself. We are now also able to approach Whitehead's treatment of the actual occasion's temporality in his sense of epochal time. We can then explore the actual occasion's feeling of the past in the perceptual mode of causal efficacy and how this makes possible the perceptual mode of presentational immediacy.

# 5

# *The Feeling of Time*

N O TRUE UNDERSTANDING OF reality is possible for Whitehead and Heidegger without an understanding of
time. In keeping with their transcendental inquiries,
Whitehead and Heidegger claim that we come to an understanding of time through our temporal experience. We can
have an interpretation of time because we "time" our involvements; we come to an interpretation of the temporal nature of
process because we feel the past flowing through us into the
future.

## *The Historical Nature of Dasein*

WHILE DEATH ILLUSTRATES Dasein's finitude, birth reveals the
profound significance of thrownness: "Factical Dasein exists
as born" (BT 426) and comes into the world with possibilities
already there and already limited. Dasein's everyday view of its
birth is simply that of one end point in a linear series of
"nows" related only by the way one point follows another. But
to understand itself as an authentic constancy of the Self, Dasein "must first *pull itself together*" (BT 441) and see that it
*"stretches along between* birth and death" (BT 425) instead
of simply occupying a segment of a time line. Dasein's initial
thrownness and Being-toward-death become unified because

of the inherent unity of temporality that allows Dasein to stretch *itself.*

The unity of temporality may be understood by a brief consideration of the constituent structures of care:

1. By existentiality, Dasein is always ahead of itself. The understanding interprets possible ways of involvement and projects those possibilities. Although primarily futural, authentic Dasein is constantly aware of and projects *from* its facticity.

2. Facticity reveals that Dasein is subject to limited, historical situations from which possibilities are drawn. As factical, authentic Dasein is always brought back to consider its past. State-of-mind discloses Dasein in its thrownness as an entity that *ontologically* has a past.

3. Absorbed in the world into which it has been thrown and upon which it is dependent, Dasein focuses upon the present and tends to cover up its past and future. As fallen, Dasein sees itself as *actual* and forgets its ownmost possibility that tempers all others.

These three elements of care are, respectively, grounded in the temporal ecstases of future, past, and present, but these ecstases are not separate, as inauthentic Dasein believes them to be. Future, past, and present are fused together as temporality temporalizes itself. J. L. Mehta writes:

> Temporality 'is' not at all an entity, but is rather a process. It 'times' or temporalizes itself *(sich zeitigt)* in its various modes. . . . Future, past, and present, involving as they do the movements respectively of 'toward oneself', 'back to', and 'encounter with' show temporality to be the *ekstatikon* pure and simple, the primordial 'standing outside itself' in and for itself.[1]

Heidegger takes great pains to show that each ecstasis, through temporalizing, includes the other two (BT 370–380). This unity of the ecstases supplies Dasein with the ability to discover a coherence in its involvements through a three-dimensional openness. Zimmerman writes that in order for the *experience* of things in time to be possible, the temporalizing activity must be inherently self-unifying. Thus Heidegger implies that the unity of temporalization is an essential *presupposition* if we are to account for the possibility of Dasein's encounter with beings.[2]

It is in this unity of involvements that Dasein may find its own unity. As inauthentic, Dasein does not recognize the ecstatic character of temporality, and its affairs are seen as scattered and unrelated. This scattered view indicates that finding this unity begins in recognizing how Dasein forfeits itself to a dispersal of events that must then be gathered up. Thus, fallenness provides the possibility of Dasein's unity being an issue at all. Without falling, there could be no distinction between an inauthentic series of nows and an authentic, temporal wholeness. It is therefore a mistake to think of authenticity as something entirely separate from everydayness, for *"authentic* existence is not something which floats above everydayness; existentially, it is only a modified way in which such everydayness is seized upon" (BT 224). Authentic Dasein pulls itself together *within* everydayness by recognizing that it is not a present-at-hand, abstract core-self but that as a self, it is an existentiell way of existing within the very world that absorbs it. To continue the spatial image of points on a line, authentic Dasein views its inauthentic self as mis-placed experiences in need of temporal unification.

As anticipatory resoluteness, authentic Dasein's concern for its potentiality is essentially futural, and since the ecstases are collapsed together by the temporalizing of temporality, future, past, and present become grounded in the future for authentic Dasein. (It is interesting to note that the German word for *future* is *Zukunft,* and in speaking of Dasein's "coming to" itself, Heidegger's term is *"Zu-kunft."*) While this temporalizing means that each temporal dimension includes features of the others, Zimmerman explains that Heidegger's treatment of the future "lies at the basis of Dasein's existence (care-moment) and its understanding (disclosedness-moment). Only insofar as Dasein opens up the horizon of the future can Dasein 'exist', i.e., understand or disclose its possibilities."[3]

Focusing upon Dasein's future projections of its own possibilities in light of Being-toward-death, as David Couzens Hoy says, "may cloud Heidegger's insistence that Dasein is not an isolated, private ego but most primordially a social, communal, and historical being."[4] It must be emphasized that a fundamental aspect of Being-in-the-world, as we have seen, is Being-with-Others. Resolute Dasein appropriates its thrownness into a world with Others in which is found Dasein's possibilities *along with* Others' potentialities for Being. Authenticity "leads rather to a recognition of the compelling situation of the actual historical world," writes Hoy.[5] What is compelling in Dasein's authentic situation is the discovery of finite possibilities presented in Being-with-Others in authentic openness. Inauthentic Dasein is unaware of the limitations essential to a historical entity. Rather than interpreting these limitations as leading to motivations of self-interest, resolute Dasein's self-concern becomes an openness *toward* the finite possibilities that are anticipated (in view of Being-toward-death) *in* Being-with-Others.

Heidegger's point is that such a self-understanding is possible only because Dasein can exist futurally (toward its potentiality) by means of the ecstatic unity of temporality. This is not to say that authenticity is a "state" of self-understanding that Dasein may "achieve." Resoluteness is an existentiell appropriation of facticity that must be repeated, and anticipation occurs only in concrete situations, not as a kind of promise to oneself. (I have avoided such terms as *behavior* and *action* to avoid suggesting that Heidegger advocates some practical good found in authentic existence.)

Dasein's authentic response to Being-with-Others is not confined to those who coexist in Dasein's lifetime, for Being-with-Others includes Dasein-that-has-been as well. The existential intentionality made possible by ecstatic temporality that allows Dasein to project future possibilities also extends to the history that is part of Dasein's facticity. Although authenticity illuminates freedom (as potentiality-for-Being [BT 237], as the result of anxiety [BT 232], and as freedom toward death [BT 311]), Dasein is not free to have a historical past other than the one it has been thrown into. Dasein is intentionally open to the past, from which possibilities can be extracted, because Dasein is essentially historical.

Although in everyday speech we talk of the historical value of artifacts, Heidegger maintains that objects per se are not historical. An artifact has historical value only as part of the world of Dasein-that-has-been; that is, the object was significantly ready-to-hand for past Dasein. What is no longer present in the artifact is that *world,* that intentional matrix of involvements, in which past Dasein found a place for the artifact. Properly speaking, Dasein can never be past with the sense of finality that can be attached to an object, for Dasein is never present-at-hand. The past may be applied as a *category* to an object, but in regard to Dasein, it must be the *existential* of having-been there *(Da-gewesen).* Since objects are not ecstatically temporal, they are historical only secondarily (BT 433) only because Dasein is primarily historical and *"only* because *it is temporal in the very base of its Being"* (BT 428).

The implication is that "history" in any sense, even as historiological, scientific study, is possible only by virtue of "its ontological derivation from Dasein's historicality" (BT 428). The past that precedes birth becomes included in the unity of Dasein's stretching along between birth and death as historicality makes this stretching possible:

> The specific movement in which Dasein is *stretched* along and stretches itself along, we call its "historizing." The question of Dasein's "connectedness" is the ontological problem of historizing. To lay bare the *structure of historizing,* and the existential-temporal conditions of its possibility, signifies that one has achieved an *ontological* understanding of *historicality.* (BT 427)

For Heidegger, history is a function not of events, people, or things that have been but of the temporal intentionality of *existing* Dasein. Heidegger's analysis of historicality is meant to show that the past is relevant to existing Dasein only because Dasein can, by means of the temporalizing of temporality, stretch itself along. The past is significant in Dasein's world as authentic temporalizing becomes authentic historizing by Dasein's appropriating and projecting itself upon possibilities that arise from having-been. Borrowing a term from Kierkegaard, Heidegger calls this process of historizing that makes history Dasein's own and is part of Dasein's ecstatic unity "repetition." History can occur because Dasein is able to open up the temporal horizons for historical events. Authentically standing out toward its potentiality, Dasein exists in a self-circling intentionality by which it is able to repeat past possibilities. Authentic Dasein uncovers and retrieves the power of Being, so to speak, in its history.

Repetition, however, is no mere parrotlike reenactment of events. Authentic historicality is the process by which the potentiality left over by Dasein-that-has-been is reclaimed by the interpretation of history, ordinarily viewed as collections of records and facts, into a reservoir of possibilities open for retrieval again and again. Inauthentically viewed, history remains simply the totality of past actuals. George J. Seidel suggests that we consider repetition a "redredging" of history, much as "one might dredge a river in order to widen the channel of its possibilities."[6] History is won back through repetition; it is, says Seidel, "a beginning originally rebegun."[7] Thus, historicality allows Dasein to open the past so that history comes to Dasein through the potentiality of the future horizon that belonged to Dasein-that-has-been. That potentiality becomes significant to Dasein as *projected;* history, therefore, is temporalized out of the future.

Through the collapse of the ecstases, the understanding telescopes this unitary temporality toward the future, so that the past becomes meaningful in light of anticipatory resoluteness. Anticipating death, Dasein is thrown back upon itself as facticity. Inauthentic Dasein, not resolutely taking up its facticity into its Being, has nothing to come back to. But as authentic, Dasein's factically given history becomes the source of resolute fulfillment of potentiality—having-been becomes futural. This is what Heidegger means in saying that "historicality will prove to be, at bottom, just a more concrete working out of temporality" (BT 434).

Historically unified into a "happening" *(Geschehen)*, Dasein's redredging of the past becomes a "waiting toward" the future, and the precise instant in which those possibilities are uncovered in Dasein's resolute projection of itself is called the "moment of vision" (Macquarrie's and Robinson's translation of *"Augenblick"*). Werner Marx writes that the moment of vision "refers to the momentous moment fraught with significance, an opportune moment *(kairos)* of resolution in which Dasein comes to terms with its total situation, especially the primordial limit situation of Being toward death."[8] In present situations, the moment of vision is the sense in which the ecstases actively interplay; Dasein is more than an entity in the particular "now" moment *(dem Jetzt)*. In the moment of vision, Dasein "re-cognizes" that it is outside of the present (and itself) in a manner that an entity simply located in space-time cannot be.

Heidegger's account of the authentic Present is quite brief and perhaps inadequate. Although the moment of vision is that existentiell event of anticipatory resoluteness in which Dasein is aware of temporalizing itself, Heidegger devotes far more text to the authentic future and having-been. In contrast, the inauthentic present receives more attention, for it is the present Dasein is absorbed into. But the brief treatment of the authentic Present does serve to underline the notion that authentic Dasein does not "spend all its time" in the present. The previous discussion of presence-at-hand as the result of focusing upon the present, actual state of a thing is relevant here. As authentic Dasein views its possibilities in terms of being temporalized in having-been, Present, and future, all Dasein's sources of possibilities can be thought of as ready-to-hand. In this manner, having-been is seen as involvable; that is, past events become significant similar to the way objects provide ready-to-hand possibilities. Dwelling only in the present, inauthentic Dasein does not recognize its ecstatic nature, so its past is not seen as a source of involvement.

To contrast the repetition of authentic having-been, inauthentic Dasein's relation to the past is one of "forgetting." The actual past is not in itself literally forgotten; what Heidegger means is that the possibilities lying in having-been are left covered up. Taking its possibilities only from its absorption in its actual, present existence, inauthentic Dasein is oblivious to its own disclosure as thrown. Dasein flees in the face of its facticity and "remembers" only the they's ambiguous, curious superficialities that are the subjects of idle talk.

To forget one's history is not to release oneself from a monolithic weight of determining factors in order to focus upon one's future, for only a resolute appropriation of having-been frees one to anticipate the potential power of the legacy of Dasein-that-has-been-there. While the present is characterized by the indifferent "making present" of inauthenticity, the authentic Present is created in the moment of vision *from* the finite field of possibilities in having-been. Again, this process of projection is possible only in an entity that is essentially futural:

> *Only an entity which, in its Being, is essentially FU-*
> *TURAL so that it is free for its death and can let itself*
> *be thrown back upon its factical "there" by shatter-*
> *ing itself against death—that is to say, only an entity*
> *which, as futural, is equiprimordially in the process*
> *of HAVING-BEEN, can by handing down to itself the*
> *possibility it has inherited, take over its thrownness*
> *and be IN THE MOMENT OF VISION for 'its time'.* (BT
> 437).

In coming to itself, Dasein does so as a type of return, but at the same time, Dasein is what it is only as it moves toward the future. This reciprocity between the future and having-been is not achieved *at* the futuremost event of death but occurs in the *process* of aiming at Dasein's ownmost possibility. This coming to itself must include *all* of Dasein's possibilities, so must occur in appropriating the thrown ground of having-been. Projectively aiming at death while appropriating all that thrownness implies *is* anticipatory resoluteness disclosed in the momentous situation of the authentic Present.

Taking up and projecting the wealth of possibilities dormant in having-been, Dasein becomes resolute toward its "heritage" (*Erbe*). In doing so, Dasein extends its thrownness beyond its birth. Dasein becomes itself not only in reaching ahead of itself to what it is not yet but also in reaching back to what it is as already passed down. This heritage, though, is always a particular heritage, a particular nationality, race, and culture with unique events, strengths, and weaknesses. This particularity means that Dasein is never Dasein *in general* but always occupying a particular point of view to interpret its history. Indeed, since the projecting function of the understanding *is* interpretation of possibility, each Dasein exists in a unique hermeneutical posture in regard to its facticity.

The intentional transformation of having-been into future projection is a process of creation in which Dasein is said to accept freely its "fate" (*Schicksals*). This fate, circling through my hermeneutical situation from the past to point the way of my future, does not determine my life, for it is a dynamic fate. Affirming my fate, I retrieve possibilities from my heritage, project them futurally, and thus in a sense am always becoming what I already am. This self-circling process of authentic Dasein arising from its heritage fatefully to meet itself exemplifies the unitary character of authentic temporality:

> The Self's resoluteness against the inconstancy of distraction, is in itself a *steadiness which has been stretched along*—the steadiness with which Dasein as fate 'incorporates' into its existence birth and death and their 'between', and holds them as thus 'incorporated', so that in such constancy Dasein is indeed in a moment of vision. (BT 442)

The discontinuity of past events, and of Dasein itself, as viewed in everydayness is unified through fate "in which Dasein *hands* itself *down* to itself, . . . a possibility it has inherited and yet chosen" (BT 435).

Another element of Dasein's authentic historizing is "destiny" (*Geschick*). Since it exists essentially as Being-with-Others, Dasein's "historizing is a co-historizing and is determinative for it as *destiny*. This is how we designate the historizing of a community, of a people. . . . Dasein's fateful destiny in and with its 'generation' goes to make up the full authentic historizing of Dasein" (BT 436). Repetition calls forth possibilities in Dasein's heritage that are interpreted *in the context* of Being-with-Others. This notion illustrates that Dasein, again, is not an isolated entity that may arbitrarily create its own historical meaning. Dasein's creative freedom for possibility is finite not only because its heritage is finite but also because its fate is limited by the collective facticity of the generation into which it is thrown. Dasein is engaged in a Dialogue with tradition in a manner possible only to an entity that exists as standing out toward its future *in order to* appropriate its history so as to come into its "own time." While its ecstatic temporality is the ground of resoluteness that makes an authentic response to destiny possible, Hoy remarks that an existential's groundedness "does not mean that something else occurs *before* destiny or fate in some genetic, causal relation—as fate before destiny, destiny before fate, or resoluteness before both—but rather that each is necessary for the other to be possible."[9]

Heidegger speaks of "a reciprocal rejoinder to the possibility of that existence which has-been there" as repetition reveals projects in fateful Dasein's heritage, and there is "at the same time a disavowal of that which in the 'today', is working itself out as the 'past'" (BT 438). "Rejoinder" seems to mean the intentional connection of Dasein to having-been that is found in the ecstatic reaching back of repetition; it asserts the fundamental inheritance of historical Dasein from Dasein-that-has-been. But "disavowal" connotes a curious attitude toward what is "working itself out." The term seems to signify the interpretive nature of Dasein's unique experiential perspective. Each act of repetition reinterprets the entire context of Dasein's heritage; history is reopened so that the possibilities of Dasein-that-has-been are linked to the self-circling unity of authentic Dasein.

For Heidegger, then, the Self is not something substantially present. In everyday idle talk, we think of ourselves as present-at-hand and attempt essentialist definitions of the Self. The result is usually a characterization of the Self as a thinking thing, an ego. Heidegger sees this sort of treatment of the Self as connected to a general tendency of equating Being with objective reality: to be is to be an object. This tendency also contributes to regarding time as a substance, an endless string of nows. For Heidegger, such a view misses the sense of the process of our existence. Authentic understanding reveals that I am a *way* to be. In the moment of vision, Dasein has the experience of a self-circling, ecstatic unity of having-been, Present, and future that is temporally spreading itself out, not happening all at once. Heidegger describes this ecstatic unity, found in authentic unity:

> Coming back to itself futurally, resoluteness brings itself into the Situation by making present. The character of "having been" arises from the future, and in such a way that the future which "has been" (or better, which "is in the process of having been") releases from itself the Present. This phenomenon has the unity of a future which makes present the process of having been; we designate it as "temporality". (BT 374)

## The Temporality of Worldhood

IT IS THE POLARITY OF, perhaps tension between, the appropriation of its past and the projection of its future made possible by ecstatic temporality that makes Dasein a historical entity. This temporal movement makes possible Dasein's ready-to-hand involvements. Zimmerman brings our attention to the temporality of worldhood:

> The question is: does our instrumental understanding of things arise from the fact that temporality lets beings show themselves as tools, or does it arise from our need to use things in order to overcome material scarcity? It does not seem to make much sense to say that beings would manifest themselves as tools except to a being (such as man) which needs tools in order to survive.[10]

The point here is that things are manifest as equipment only by the involvements that Dasein has with them. It is not the temporality of the things themselves that makes this possible but the temporality of Dasein. Dasein indeed needs tools, but the ability to be involved with tools is due to the recognition of the equipmental possibilities of things and the power to project these possibilities in involvements. This projection is made possible by Dasein's ability to "await" and to "retain." Through circumspection, Dasein retains its past encounters with tools. The experiences are retained not in the sense of memories but as possibilities that are awaited as future possibilities.

For example, I recognize the utensil in front of me to be a pen because of my past use of pens. I reach for the pen when I wish to write because I expect a certain response from the pen when it is moved across the paper. Because I am a temporal being, the significant involvements of my past are available to me as possibilities for the future. Through retaining and awaiting, I am able to bring about an actual involvement in the present. The pen is made manifest as ready-to-hand because I have awaited and retained. As Joseph P. Fell writes, "[A] hammer is (now) a hammer as an instrument for the (future) end of hammering, and the hammer already is (past) a member of the class of tools that can be used for this purpose."[11]

It should be noted that this account of retaining and awaiting as providing the temporal ground of involvement repeats a crucial theme of *Being and Time,* the unitary circling nature of past, present, and future. As Being-in-the-world, Dasein finds itself already in a complex of involvements. Dasein retains past involvements and uses them to discover tools in the present situation. As past involvements belong to Dasein, so do future possible involvements that arise from what is retained. The past and the future merge upon each other as retaining and awaiting actualize a present encounter.

Again, Heidegger has very little to say about the present in which the encounter actually takes place. Given his emphasis of possibility over actuality, however, Heidegger accordingly spends his energy discussing retaining, which is the source of possible involvements, and awaiting, which is the projection of those possibilities. He makes it clear that we can have no understanding of how Dasein has significant relations with tools unless we consider the unitary character of temporality. To offer a lengthy account of the present would give undue stress to actuality and would make it easy to lose sight of the past and future. Such forgetfulness is more difficult, Heidegger seems to say, when we try to consider the past or future alone. When we think of past involvements, we are somehow forced to think of those involvements as repeatable in the future. Similarly, in imagining future experiences with things, we recognize that these images are modeled upon past experience. But to focus attention upon the present leads us to think of objects *as they are* at this moment. Possible involvements are not in mind. When the past and future fade from view, things are seen as present-at-hand and without significance. Thus Heidegger finds it sufficient to remark that in encountering entities, the present is the bringing together of awaiting and retaining.

Suppose that the pen runs out of ink and thereby becomes conspicuous. While I no longer project future pen involvements, I may take a moment to turn the pen about in my hand and contemplate it as a piece of matter. Viewing the malfunctioning pen qua object without considering past encounters or future possibilities, the threefold unity of temporality that made possible its readiness-to-hand seems no longer to operate. What is it about my Being that makes this presence-at-hand mode possible? Heidegger shows that it also is my temporality.

We have already seen how conspicuousness, obtrusiveness, and obstinacy can call up the present-at-hand mode, and the temporality of these occurrences has also been discussed. But those conditions are not necessary for me to shift my view from the utensil nature of a hammer. This shift of my relation to the object brings up a discussion of praxis and theory. In the praxis of involvement, Dasein makes use of "deliberating" in which an "if-then" schema is formulated. *If* a certain action is performed with an instrument, *then* a certain result will follow. This schema is not to be construed in a logical sense but in the temporal sense of *when* the action is performed, *thereafter* a result follows.

It is apparent that this if-then schema is due to retaining-awaiting, which is not found in the theoretical mode of presence-at-hand. But even though "the ontological possibility of 'theory' will be due to the *absence of praxis*—that is, to a *privation,"* the two are not totally distinct, for "just as *praxis* has its own kind of sight ('theory'), theoretical research is not without a praxis of its own" (BT 409). The difference between the two is that theory, as "an *existential conception of science"* (BT 408), requires that Dasein transcend what the theory is about. While praxis remains prethematic, theory is a thematizing activity in which that which does the thematizing is not part of what is thematized.

Dasein must "step out of" the world to consider objects in their presence-at-hand. While the Kantian flavor of this account is evident, Heidegger's notion of transcendence relies upon the horizons of the ecstases of past, present, and future. (It is important to remember that *ecstasis* means "to stand out.") The temporal horizons of significance are as follows: (1) A tool is significant to Dasein futurally in that the tool is for-the-sake-of Dasein's benefit to perform a future task. (2) The tool is significant in-the-face-of-which Dasein finds itself. The facticity of the past is already in the world of Dasein's relational involvements. (3) In the actual situations of using instruments, a tool becomes an in-order-to that is manipulated in the present to accomplish a task now.

Michael Gelven summarizes how these horizons allow Dasein to transcend:

> To transcend means to "go beyond." But there must be some "place" to go. Transcendence, then, is possible only because there are ekstases. But ekstases do not "step out" to nowhere; they must have horizons. The horizons, though, are temporal in character. Hence, to transcend is possible only because we are temporal.[12]

While not going to the lengths Kant did in accounting for the possibility of scientific inquiry, Heidegger provides what he believes is enough for us to understand that the thematizing of entities within-the-world presupposes Being-in-the-world as the basic state of Dasein. . . . And if Dasein's Being is completely grounded in temporality, then temporality must make possible Being-in-the-world and therewith Dasein's transcendence; this transcendence in turn provides the support for concernful Being alongside entities within-the-world, whether this Being is theoretical or practical. (BT 415)

Thus, Dasein intends and transcends its world through ecstatic temporality.

So far, we have seen that Dasein's temporality makes involvements possible and that Dasein may exist in an interpretation of its temporality as ecstatic, finite unity, but we have not examined Heidegger's notion of time itself. For Heidegger, we have an idea of time in the ordinary sense only *because* we exist as ecstatic temporality. It is this element in Heidegger's transcendental inquiry that is perhaps the crucial theme running through *Being and Time*. Later we shall see that in a similar way for Whitehead, our sense of time as such is possible because of our *feeling* of time within ourselves. Now I turn to Heidegger's explanation of how our understanding of time itself is derived from our temporality.

## *Time*

ALTHOUGH WE SPEAK OF ENTITIES other than Dasein as being in time, they are not temporal in the sense that Dasein is: they do not project futurally, they do not retrieve possibilities from having-been and so on. These objects are, however, encountered by Dasein in situations, and Dasein understands its involvements as happening earlier, later, or now. These obvious temporal dimensions that we find in carrying out our daily affairs are the means by which our involvements are "dated," although this datability does not mean marks on a calendar. What is not so obvious, Heidegger points out, is exactly what we mean by such terms as *earlier, ago, later, before, then*.

These terms do not belong to things themselves, although nearly all of our discourse about things implicitly refers to when they are encountered. The reason for this datability lies in Dasein's process of awaiting and retaining that makes possible any encounters at all. Ecstatically open to the world of the ready-to-hand, Dasein awaits what will happen "then," retains what happened "ago," and is therefore able to encounter things "now."

The concernful encounters with the world made possible by the awaiting-retaining process provides our primary experience of time. The datability of our immediate experience reflects our ecstatic in-time-ness that makes possible an understanding of time as such. Dasein's ability to date involvements provides the opportunity to attempt to measure time by a timepiece. Heidegger believes that our most common measurement of time—day and night—is closely tied to our ordinary involvements: day is a time to work, and night is a time to rest. Measuring time by the position of the sun is a natural way of determining how much time is left to continue to work until darkness interrupts. Unable to see well at night, we take the opportunity to rest. More precise measurements of worktime are provided by the sundial and the clock. Noting the movements of the sundial's shadow or the clock's hands, we gauge a series of now moments in the datability of worldhood: it is twelve o'clock—now it is time to eat; it is three o'clock—now it is time to leave.

The spatial relation between the moving pointer of the clock's hands and the clock's face represents a view of time as a series of instants, much as Aristotle spoke of time as the number of motion in the *Physics*. Seeing time as this infinite, unstoppable march of moments reflects Dasein's forgetting that this "public time," useful in discourse with Others, arises from the practical need to date involvements. Instead, public time becomes understood as a present-at-hand substance whose ground in Dasein's datability is covered up. Absorption in everyday concerns leads to the belief that time is drawn from a bottomless reservoir with innumerable "nows" at everyone's access. The significance of dating worldly encounters, grounded in Dasein's temporality, is covered up.

The everyday view of public time is related to inauthenticity because

1. The discussion above indicated that the ability to time worldly experience is grounded in Dasein's datability but that this existential feature is forgotten in the absorption in Being-alongside entities, that is, fallenness. Not to recognize datability is not to recognize Dasein's temporality, which makes datability possible, and inauthenticity *is* the covering up of the meaning of Dasein's Being as care.

2. Public time is seen as a linear procession of now moments; hence, the ecstatic, nonlinear nature of temporality is hidden.

3. These nows are thought to be individual substances, appearing and passing away as material objects do. The present moment is considered just another element added to experience and not what brings the experience to be.

4. The procession of nows is understood to be infinite, and thus Dasein's finitude is covered up; attention is drawn away from Dasein's ownmost possibility of death. The connection between the public view of time and the idle talk of the they in which the inevitability of one's death is ignored is apparent.

5. Time is seen to belong "to everyone—and that means to nobody" (BT 477); thus, public time obstructs Dasein's sense of mineness.

In spite of these reasons for public time's connection to inauthenticity, it is ironically true, Heidegger points out, that even in "the kind of talk which emphasizes time's passing away, the *finite futurity* of Dasein's temporality is publicly reflected" (BT 478). The platitudes Heidegger refers to are central to the idle talk that covers up understanding that otherwise could reveal that Dasein's temporality makes possible any view of time, even an inauthentic view. Given that public time is understood as an endless stream of moments, instead of saying that time passes away, we could "say with *just as much* emphasis that it arises" (BT 478). Most often, a remark about time's passing signifies an attitude of regret about time's unstoppable march, and mentioning time's arising is less common probably because it more powerfully stresses this irrepressible movement. Heidegger's idea here is that Dasein "understands, in the end, more of time than it wants to admit," for our primordial experience of the world, although not always completely explicit, is temporal, but "the halting of time is something that we want" (BT 478).

Two important points can be drawn here. First, in speaking of time's passing or arising, the inauthentic view implicitly, and perhaps lamentably, includes a reference to time's unstoppable march, a march that Dasein somehow wants to halt. Why does Dasein want to halt time? Heidegger claims that it is because the movement of time reminds Dasein of its approaching death. As discussed earlier, the they constantly avoids facing death, but this does not mean that we are ever convinced that we are immortal. The constant covering up of death occurs precisely because we always know "deep down" that we are going to die. The idle talk designed to cover up death (among other things) endlessly struggles against our every experience, for we always have some vague awareness that we are pulled toward the future in which lies death. Thus, the inauthentic understanding that attempts to evade death leads to an inauthentic view of time.

Second, the fact that time is said to pass away (or to arise) includes a vague understanding of the dynamic process that is Dasein's temporality. This fact is in keeping with Heidegger's phenomenological hermeneutic of disclosing what is already implicit in our experience in contrast to offering solutions to problems. Just as the whole of *Being and Time* (again, a portion of a much larger projected work) aims to clarify what we already know about Being, each topic Heidegger takes up is one that, he claims, we already nebulously comprehend. In this case we all know, in some sense, what we mean by "time," but to unpack this meaning requires tortuous examination.

Heidegger's discussion of time as such is quite brief, and he does not claim that his phenomenological, painstaking journey has brought us to a clear concept of time. He does claim that he has uncovered finite, ecstatic temporality as the meaning of Dasein's Being. Such a dis-covery is a grand, if incomplete, achievement toward providing an authentic understanding of time as such. He suggests on the last page of *Being and Time* that Dasein's temporality may lead to the disclosure of time as the horizon of Being. Further analysis may show, somehow, that Temporality *(Temporalität)* is the meaning of Being, as temporality *(Zeitlichkeit)* is the meaning of care. We have seen that Heidegger considers the entity Dasein a concrete, historical openness to possibility brought about by a process of finite, ecstatic temporality. Heidegger suggests, then, that the larger work he envisioned may show that just as temporality is the meaning of this concrete openness, which is Dasein, time is the meaning of Being, the openness as such that is the ground of any opening toward any possibility.

## *The Epochal Theory of Time*

EARLIER WE SAW THAT ACTUAL occasions are essentially temporal perspectives upon the world. The temporality of actual occasions provides the fundamental units of time itself. Heidegger claims that our inauthentic and authentic understandings of time derive from inauthentic and authentic understandings of Dasein's temporality. Whitehead makes a much more radical claim: Actual occasions are temporal atoms, each an undivided epoch with no temporal, internal phases. After examining this epochal theory of time, I can move to a discussion of perception that may be applied more easily to experience on the human level than the descriptions of the previous chapter.

We have primitive feelings of time in the mode of causal efficacy in which the weight of the past presses upon us in vague yet concrete bodily experiences. These are feelings of the "great dark ocean of existence" to which Santayana refers. Because of these perceptions of causal efficacy, we are able to experience the "superficial lights" of presentational immediacy, the clear yet in a sense abstract perceptions that have received most attention from philosophers and that we usually take to be our basic experiences of the world. Finally, through symbolic reference, sometimes called a mixed mode of perception, we are able to have spatial experience of the contemporary world.

Whitehead claims that it follows from his description of concrescence that an actual occasion "is the enjoyment of a certain quantum of physical time" (PR 283). We might expect that each separate prehension is a temporal unit, but Whitehead claims that the life of the actual occasion, although it may be abstractly analyzed into phases, is not divided into earlier and later temporal parts. The actual occasion happens at once in a moment of becoming. Each occasion prehends its data, conceptually reproduces these prehensions, undergoes transmutation, has conscious feelings, and so on as an undivided, temporal whole. Rather than a series of instants, time is a supersession of epochs. Instead of flowing, process pulsates. This is the general meaning of "there is a becoming of continuity, but no continuity of becoming" (PR 35).

Whitehead argues for his epochal notion of time by drawing from Zeno's paradoxes. The paradox of the arrow, which Zeno intended as a proof that motion is an illusion, is adapted to illustrate that there cannot be temporal moments within moments. The arrow paradox is often interpreted to show that since the arrow must traverse half the distance to its target, then half the remaining distance, then half of that distance, and so on, the arrow can never complete its flight. Whitehead's point is that if the flight of the arrow, taken as a concrescence, is divided into such phases, it can never *begin* its flight. To posit temporal phases amounts to treating the phases as if there were actual occasions within actual occasions. In such a mistaken view, an actual occasion could come into being only after an infinite succession of phases, themselves actual occasions.

The view of time that is vulnerable to Zeno's paradox rests upon two assumptions: "(i) that in every becoming something (*res vera*) becomes, and (ii) that every act of becoming is divisible into earlier and later sections which are themselves acts of becoming" (PR 68). A contradiction holds between these two assumptions, for the something in (i) could never become if it must become in earlier and later sections, as mentioned in (ii). A second of becoming, by (ii), contains an earlier half second, which contains an earlier quarter second, ad infinitum. By this, the becoming of any "creature we indicate presupposes an earlier creature which became after the beginning of the second and antecedently to the earlier creature" (PR 68). But the view fails, for nothing could become "so as to effect a transition into the second in question" (PR 68).

Whitehead's solution to the puzzle is to claim that temporal extendedness becomes but that its becoming is not extended; occasions become as epochs with no succession of earlier or later parts. We can consider the entire flight of the arrow one actual occasion. It is not the arrow that receives attention, for it is the flight that is the metaphor for becoming. Intellectually, the beginning of the flight can be separated from its end, but the actual trajectory is actual only as a whole. To think of the flight as actually divided is to commit the fallacy of misplaced concreteness.

The difficulty of conceiving this epochal theory of becoming is aggravated by Whitehead's apparent inconsistency. For instance, he writes that "concrescence is divisible into an initial stage of many feelings, and a succession of subsequent phases of more complex feelings interpreting the earlier simpler feeling, up to the satisfaction which is one complex unity of feeling" (BT 220). Whitehead calls such descriptions of these "phases" the "genetic analysis" of concrescence. Yet he also writes that the "datum of internal relations makes it impossible to attribute 'change' to any actual entity" (PR 58–59). If actual occasions are considered temporally atomic, it may make sense to say that actual occasions do not change, but a genetic analysis of phases within concrescence seems to assume some sort of internal change. At the same time, Whitehead writes that in concrescence "there is a succession of phases in which new prehensions arise by integration of prehensions in antecedent phases" (PR 26). Also, an actual occasion "is a process from phase to phase, each phase being the real basis from which its successor proceeds towards the completion of the thing in question" (PR 215). Again, the becoming of the actual occasion "can be analyzed genetically into a series of subordinate phases which presuppose their antecedents" (PR 154). If there is no outright contradiction among these passages, there is at least something strange about speaking of temporal phases of a temporal whole.

A number of commentators have noted this difficulty. Christian has written that if we are to accept that the phases of concrescence can be in any way prior to other phases, it must be a priority "of its own kind," unlike any other.[13] V. C. Chappell's "Whitehead's Theory of Becoming" is less sympathetic, arguing that the epochal theory of concrescence is unintelligible and that Whitehead's modification of Zeno's argument is invalid.[14] While Chappell's essay maintains that Whitehead's theory is better off without the notion of temporal epochs, David A. Sipfle has argued against Chappel and claimed that the epochal theory is not only intelligible but necessary to Whitehead's thought.[15]

Perhaps what is in need of revision is not the epochal theory but the somewhat careless language of the numerous ill-fitting passages that create the problem. Stated more clearly, perhaps the presentation of the theory could more precisely express the way "analysis of a actual entity is only intellectual" (PR 227). In an actual occasion of a concrete human experience, we may see the sense in which the experience "is divisible; but is in fact undivided" (PR 227). A nice example is provided by Wallack:[16] When we hold an object in our hands, say a stone, we may intellectually abstract a number of features in the experience. There is the feeling of the shape of the stone, the feeling of the weight of the stone, a sense of the warmth or coolness of the stone, and so on. In addition, we may feel pleasure in the smoothness of the stone but discomfort in the stone's heaviness. Also, we sense the configuration of the fingers around the stone, the angle of the wrist, and the extension of the arm. Similarly, we may have visual experience of the stone in which we see its shape, size, color, and distance from the eyes, and perhaps find the sight appealing or annoying. Each of these cases might be interpreted as a single actual occasion. Wallack writes, however, that "there is not first a feeling of smoothness or roughness . . . then afterwards a feeling of like or dislike . . . then after that a feeling of an aim to hold a stone in the hand having been fulfilled."[17]

The hand-on-stone experience involves more facets than the rough genetic analysis above. First, the stone is a nexus of occasions prehending one another to form an enduring object that can be prehended in a single experience (involving mutually prehended eternal objects in a transmuted feeling). For that matter, the hand too is a nexus.[18] Moreover, this experience is of a special type, for it involves conscious feeling. But even with these complexities, the hand-on-stone experience is one experience. At this level, we have an instance of the happening of an actual occasion that is phenomenologically available. While holding the stone, I am certainly aware of a number of the many features of the experience—the stone's shape, size, my pleasure or dislike of the experience, and so on. But I *feel* all of these components *as* parts of the same vague experience.

This simultaneity of feeling appears to be even more true of the hand-on-stone experience if it occurs in the mode of readiness-to-hand. If I reach for and grab a rock to use as a weapon or as a makeshift hammer, my conscious experience may distinguish a temporal succession of first a feeling of coolness in the split second that my fingers make the initial contact, then a sensation of roughness as I tighten my grip, then a sensation of the stone's weight as I lift it, and so on. But is it not perhaps the case that I can distinguish such successive phases only *after* my involvement with the rock? After the ready-to-hand engagement, I may abstractly consider the actual completed experience. If that is the case, then I reflect upon the experience as present-at-hand and am no longer involved in the *becoming* of the event.

But is it not the case that I experience the rock encounter

*as taking time?* While it is true that I feel all the features of the rock and perhaps have emotional attitudes about it at the same time, might I not feel these features at the same time *for a while,* in the same way that I can see the shape, size, and color of the rock *for a while?* In other words, if Whitehead is right, must I believe that my experience with the rock took no time? Indeed, Whitehead writes that "genetic passage from phase to phase is not in physical time" (PR 283). We cannot expect, it seems, to experience the temporal growth of singular events in concrescence, for "physical time expresses some features of the growth, but *not* the growth of the features" (PR 283).

What features of concrescence, then, are expressed by physical time? Whitehead supplies a possible answer in stating that "physical time makes its appearance in the 'coordinate' analysis of the 'satisfaction'" (PR 283). "Coordinate analysis" refers to relations between actual occasions, so it seems that time occurs between a satisfied actual occasion and another. Thus, an actual occasion is in time only after it has perished. On this point, Wallack comments "that physical time is found only by retrospective analysis of an actual occasion . . . by comparing it to other occasions."[19] The implication is that the sorts of things that can be before or after one another can be only satisfied actual occasions, not the feelings within actual occasions. Whatever sort of duration takes place within the temporal extension of concrescence must be a nonlinear succession producing satisfaction through which arises the temporally extended world.

My temporal experience of the hand-on-stone event must therefore be an experience of a succession of satisfactions. The reason why I do not feel the individual satisfactions following one another is that the actual occasions are not simply lined up like beads on a string, for the intentional, vector character of a perished occasion entering objective immortality transfers the previous satisfaction *into* succeeding actual occasions. Temporal events are not merely before or after one another, "for time is cumulative as well as reproductive" (PR 283). Feeling the stone is feeling a historical summary. As Kraus puts it, "Time is perpetually growing in 'extensity,' not in 'length,' in the same manner as that in which memory is continually growing in the richness of its content."[20]

The intentionality of the actual occasion by which it is thrust into objective immortality makes possible the cumulative nature of time. Time does not merely flow—it builds up. For this reason, epochs cannot be thought of as the "nows" of a linear view of time that Heidegger criticizes. Heidegger warns that we misunderstand time (and ourselves and Being) when we think of it as temporal units arranged one after another. The ecstases of having-been, present, and future stand out from themselves and enter into one another. Whitehead's epochs are units, but units that grow into others. This is why actual occasions are said to be in transition: they are in transit into new becomings.

Unaware of the actual occasion's "real potentiality which is referent beyond itself" (PR 72), we commit the fallacy of misplaced concreteness implicit in a Newtonian view that considers time a substance apart from and *in* which events occur (PR 70–72). This mistake occurs when we make a generalization from our observations of enduring, material objects (PR 35) and do not recognize that such an object is a "historical route of actual occasions" (PR 321). Heidegger expresses the same idea in saying that we get this ordinary notion of time from our derivative present-at-hand mode of perception while ignoring our primary, temporal involvement with the ready-to-hand. The Newtonian view ignores the potentiality essential to every event. The authentic view of time for Whitehead is, as Christian writes, "'time lived' not 'time measured'."[21]

## Causal Efficacy

WHITEHEAD DISCUSSES THE IDEA of lived time through his analysis of perception in the mode of causal efficacy. Actual occasions do not simply feel past occasions; past actual occasions are felt *as* past. This fact is not always clear in our experience. Just as Heidegger argues that we tend to treat our present-at-hand view as primary, Whitehead argues that we often equate human perception with the clear and distinct ideas found in the mode of presentational immediacy. Western philosophy has adopted this dogma, and epistemological theory has focused upon immediate, conscious experience while ignoring the *more* immediate, vague feelings of the world. For Whitehead, presentational immediacy, though derived from feelings of causal efficacy, is a highly abstractive function of sensing the present, but this manner of perceiving "gives no information as to the past or the future" (PR 168). To consider presentational immediacy the primary (more commonly the sole) manner of perception is to be unable to form a sense of our own temporality as experienced. In that case, all that is left is to make an analogy with enduring objects perceived in presentational immediacy.

The vague feelings of temporality found in causal efficacy provide the ground for Causality. Whitehead uses Hume's search for an impression of a necessary, causal connection to illustrate the failure of presentational immediacy to provide an experience of an event's coming to be. Hume was correct, according to Whitehead, in maintaining that all of our ideas come from immediate sensations, but Hume's mistake was to restrict immediate sensation to presentational immediacy. Hume concluded that we have no impressions of necessary connections and that our idea of causality is derived from habit, and insofar as his analysis was restricted to presentational immediacy, Hume was correct (PR 123). To avoid what Santayana has called "the solipsism of the present moment" to which Hume's position leads, we must "include in direct perception something more that presentational immediacy" (PR 81).

What must be included is a kind of bodily experience distinct from the perceptions that come through the five senses. Attributing our information about worldly involvement to the five senses, especially vision, results in a representational epistemology that in turn fosters subject-object dualism. This representational, dualistic view can tell us only that perceived objects have extension and are "implicated in a complex of extended relatedness with the animal body of the percipient"

(PR 122). A representational theory cannot explain how we know much more about the world—for instance, our knowledge of causality. With the representational theory, says Kraus, "the experient becomes permanently locked in the movie theater of the mind, endlessly watching a parade of images essentially unconnected either with each other or with an external, active world."[22]

Rejecting perceptual representationalism, Whitehead opts for a theory of perception in which perceived objects are not just mirrored in the percipient but are revealed in their immanence in the experiencer. This immanence is ontologically prior to our perception of those objects, for it is "implicitly assumed in every detail of our organization of life" (PR 79). Again, Whitehead's transcendental approach is evident. Whitehead's philosophy of organism is indeed a pluralism, and it is necessary to any pluralism that individual events transcend one another in some ways. Presentational immediacy is our means of perceiving this transcendence, but at the expense of overlooking our Being-in-the-world. By means of causal efficacy, "there is a disclosure of objectified data, which are *known as* having a *community* with the immediate experience for which they are data" (PR 79, stress added).

We do not perceive objects and afterward deduce causal connections between them; as the data of experience are disclosed through causal efficacy, the "mutual implication" (PR 79) involved is revealed in the experience. Thus, Whitehead contends that causal efficacy, the mode of perception that includes a feeling of the actual occasion's intentional ability to enter into the constitution of another, is more fundamental than presentational immediacy. Therefore, a thorough perceptual theory must be a theory about this intentionality: "The problem of perception and the problem of power are one and the same" (PR 58).

While our clear, vivid sensations lack reference to the past and future, we directly feel the movement of the past into the future in our "vague, haunting, unmanageable" experiences.[23] A systematic theory of causality must accept or contend with Hume's claim that we induce the future's conformity to the past through the repeated temporal juxtaposition of similar sensa, but for Whitehead, any such theory presupposes some vague sense of conformity not found in the sensa (of presentational immediacy). We feel the conformity of the future to the past in those vague experiences in which the world weighs upon us:

> In the dark there are vague presences, doubtfully feared; in the silence, the irresistible causal efficacy of nature presses itself upon us; in the vagueness of the low hum of insects in an August woodland, the inflow into ourselves of feelings from enveloping nature over- whelms us; in the dim consciousness of half-sleep, the presentations of sense fade away, and we are left with the vague feeling of influences from vague things around us. (PR 176).

Whitehead offers an example of a direct, literal feeling that leads us to believe that the future will conform to the past. A light is switched on, and a man who was previously in the darkness sees the flash and blinks his eyes. A highly sophisticated account can be given from the current in the electrical wiring, the resistance of the filament in the bulb, the reflection of light upon the retinae, and so on, to the contraction of the muscles in the eyelids. But if the man is asked about his *experience,* he will explain that the flash *made* him blink. If pressed about how he knows that the flash made him blink, the man will say that he knows because he *felt* the flash make him blink. The Humean may insist that the man had no impression of the flash's causing him to blink but only an impression of the flash followed by a feeling of "his habit of *blinking* after flashes" (PR 175). But if habits can be felt, asks Whitehead, why not causes? We do not suspect that there are causal influences between events and thereby look for cases of causality and devise theories. Rather, the "notion of causation arose because mankind lives amid experiences in the mode of causal efficacy" (PR 175).

Whitehead's answer to the question How is it possible for one thing to cause another? is an appeal to the most fundamental nature of process, the vector character of prehensions. Vectors are the primordial movements of the world by which the past moves into the present and the present into the future. To say that A caused B is to assert that A was an event that perished in the past of B and has moved into the becoming of B. This temporal intentionality of feelings makes it possible that "we finish a sentence *because* we have begun it" (PR 129). We feel our past pressing upon us, and as Kraus writes, we receive an "im-pression" from the past in our present that we in turn "ex-press" to the future.[24] Feeling the world pour through us in this temporal transition provides our vague experiences of causality out of which we can begin to construct theories of causal efficacy, which means that this feeling of vector movements

> produces the sense of derivation from an immediate past, and of passage to an immediate future; a sense of emotional feeling, belonging to oneself in the past, passing into oneself in the present, and passing from oneself in the present towards oneself in the future. . . . This is our general sense of existence. (PR 178)

Heidegger tells us that we come to an authentic "general sense of existence" in the moment of vision when we know ourselves to be a temporal process of resolutely appropriating potentiality from having-been and anticipating the projection of ourselves into the future toward death, yet remaining as potentiality to be appropriated by future Dasein. Similarly for Whitehead, the present *is* that moment of appropriating the potentiality of what is given and anticipating the satisfaction of the moment as providing potential to be appropriated by superseding occasions. The past *is* that given world of potentiality. The future *is* that anticipated prehension of what is now becoming but soon will be given for subsequent actual occasions.

The paradigm case of this temporal movement of the world into the actual occasion is our primitive perception of "feeling the body as functioning" (PR 81). It is a simple yet easily overlooked fact that "we feel with the body" (PR 311). Our conscious experiences are always in some manner experiences of bodily involvement, for "our bodies are largely contrivances whereby some central actual occasion may inherit these basic experiences of its antecedent parts" (PR 178–79). The human body is a nexus, and a conscious event has its "nearest" environment in the activities of the brain. This environment extends to larger ones that include the events of the nervous system, the hand that holds the stone, the forest that contains the stone and the person, and so on. What occurs, then, are overlapping historical routes of transferences of feelings for which "the human body is to be conceived as a complex 'amplifier'" (PR 119). By the amplification of the vectors of these historical routes, "we essentially arise out of our bodies which are the stubborn facts of the immediate relevant past" (PR 129).

Since conscious events acquire their contents from the *"withness* of the body" (PR 64), the body is "the starting point for knowledge of the circumambient world" (PR 81). Heidegger's favorite examples of Dasein's involvement with the world concern our use of objects, no doubt because of the intimacy we experience with tools. In our ready-to-*hand* relationship with a hammer, we must pick up, hold, and swing the hammer with the hand. We grip the hammer *with* the hand, we watch it strike the nail *with* the eye, and we hear the metals meet *with* the ear. If we feel the hammer's weight and judge it too heavy for use, the conspicuousness of the object highlights the anticipated hammering that should have fit the strength in the hand and arm. For Whitehead, such involvement illustrates our most basic case of sense *re*ception. We can perceive the environment because we can receive its data, and our original sense of this perception comes through bodily involvement.

The disclosure of the world through the body is possible because the body is a "highly organized and immediate part of the general environment" (PR 119) with vague parameters not easily distinguished from the wider complex of objects. Those portions of the physical world with which we are less involved, from which there is less sense reception, are the more remote parts of the environment, while what is most intimate and immediate is the bodily organs. Through our experience in the bodily organs, we conform "to the vague world which lies beyond them."[25] Although it is true, Whitehead admits, that our thematic understanding of the living body must be interpreted by the same general scientific principles by which we understand other elements of the universe, there is another side of this principle, "for it carries with it the converse deduction that other sections of the universe are to be interpreted in accordance with what we know of the human body" (PR 119). Here we find one of Whitehead's more explicit statements concerning his transcendental inquiry: Since we have direct experiences of the presence of the world in the withness of the body, we can form a worldview based upon this process of appropriation.

In summary, we can have an understanding of causality because we can experience the inheritance of the past by the present (and the projection of the present into the future). This inheritance is possible by the fundamental, creative intentionality of concrescence that is its temporal movement. Is this movement of one thing into another phenomenologically available? Yes—through the experience of causal efficacy in the body: "The feeling *of* the stone *is* in the *hand;* the feeling *of* the food is the ache *in the stomach*" (PR 118).

Whitehead's treatment of causal efficacy has focused upon the perception of the movement of the past into the present. The other side of this movement, how the inheritance of the past endows experience with power to project, needs to be examined in terms of human experience, and we shall see another aspect of the transcendental inquiry. For Whitehead, the primitive, concrete experience of causal efficacy *makes possible* the derived, more abstract experience of presentational immediacy. As Heidegger claims that our spatiality is *made possible* by temporality, we shall see that causal efficacy, which gives us our feeling of time, *makes possible* presentational immediacy, by which we come to a sense of space.

# 6

# *The Now and the There*

## *The Extensive Continuum*

**P**ERCEPTION IN THE MODE OF causal efficacy, like Heidegger's moods, provides us with immediate feelings of the weight of the world. In the vague feelings of the past, we experience the creative advance of process in a manner more fundamental than our visual and auditory images. In contrast to these heavy, imprecise sensations, we also have perceptions that are "distinct, controllable, apt for immediate enjoyment, and with minimum reference to past, or to future" (PR 179). Such perceptions are not felt to be of the past but of what appears to us in the present. These are the perceptions belonging to the mode of presentational immediacy that provides us with a sense of our spatial relations to objects in the contemporary world. We shall see that these perceptions of presentational immediacy are "impure," though, for they derive from the "pure" prehensions of causal efficacy found in the withness of the body (PR 63–64). In the context of the transcendental inquiry, we shall see that it is possible to understand our experiences of the presentationally immediate only because we can understand prior, causal feelings: the clear is made possible by the vague.

This derivation has a rough parallel in the relationship of presence-at-hand to readiness-at-hand. Dasein's primordial experience is based upon the temporal awaiting and retaining of direct involvement with the world, while Dasein's derivative relations of presence-at-hand concern the mere appearance of objects with no reference to the past or the future. However, Dasein can have present-at-hand experiences only because of its ability to have ready-to-hand involvements. Causal efficacy expresses the worldliness of the world as the actual occasion directly feels its involvement in the world while the past moves into and through the actual occasion. Presentational immediacy takes information from those worldly feelings and constructs images of the present world without reference to the past or the future. In a very broad manner of speaking, since it is a derivative mode of experience and illustrates the abstract character of things apart from the experiencer's intimate practical involvement, presentational immediacy is in some ways Whitehead's version of presence-at-hand. While these loose parallels will be referred to again, the comparison probably cannot be drawn much further. What is important here is that presentationally immediate perceptions are possible only to an entity that becomes through its intentional appropriations of past occasions.

We have seen that actual occasions prehend only their antecedents. It follows that contemporary actual occasions, although prehending the same actual world (while making allowances for their unique perspectives on that world), must be mutually independent—contemporaries do not prehend each other. This independence of contemporaries is also demanded by the fact that actual occasions are finite by virtue of their attainment of satisfaction. Since satisfaction is a completely determinate feeling of subjective unity, the actual occasion must be able to achieve closure. If contemporary occasions provided additional data to be prehended, the actual occasion could never reach satisfaction. It may seem, then, that actual occasions could have no perceptions of the contemporary world. Indeed, for Whitehead, to say that two occasions are contemporaries means that neither has physical prehensions of the other. This definition of *contemporary* is in keeping with the tenets of relativity physics.[1] But how is it that although I may accept Whitehead's claim that I do not perceive present actualities, I still know that my experience is directly related to what is occurring *now?* Whitehead's answer is that while causal efficacy provides feelings of the appropriation of past *actualities,* presentational immediacy is the actual occasion's way of perceiving what is presently *potential.* Perceiving regions of potentiality, the actual occasion experiences what Whitehead calls the "extensive continuum."

Whitehead's emphasis on potentiality over actuality is especially evident in his idea of the consideration of all actual occasions' perspectives in terms of "one relational complex" that "underlies the whole world, past, present, and future" (PR 66). This relational complex is the extensive continuum, "a scheme of real potentiality" that provides the possible conditions of extensiveness out of which actual occasions arise (PR 76–77). While the past is composed of satisfied actualities, each a determinate perspective on the experienceable world, the present is filled with potential "places" for the becomings of occasions. Since these perspectives are yet indeterminate, the concrescing actual occasion occurs within a continuum of perspectives. Past actual occasions incorporate the relations of a pluralistic network of mutual prehensions, yet the concrescing actual occasion feels these past actual occasions in their atomic character as satisfied units of many feelings. But the contemporary world, lacking this *actual* atomic character, is a field of *potential,* perspectival atomizings of the extensive continuum. Concrescence happens in a region of possible, extensive relations among contemporary becomings.

What must be explained is how contemporary actual occasions can occupy unique perspectives, become in unchanging temporal units, have no physical perhensions of each other, and yet belong to and perceive a common world. If the universe were some sort of receptacle in which actual occasions occur, we would have a device for explaining the relations among contemporaries. But such a receptacle would be actual and prior to actual occasions, thereby violating the ontological principle. Whitehead opts for an abstract scheme based upon the actual occasion's fundamental intentionality: "The primary *relationship* of physical occasions is *extensive connection"* (PR 288), and this connection coordinates contemporaries through their extensity toward potential divisions of regions into possible perspectives. The extensive continuum, then, "expresses the solidarity of all possible standpoints throughout the whole process of the world" (PR 66).

The contemporary world is not yet atomic and actual, but it is possible because of the general *intentionality* of the experiences of atomizing concrescences. This "atomization of the extensive continuum is also its temporalization," for "embracing the actual past and the potential future" is the essential, appetitious "positive experience of each actual entity" (PR 72). A transcendental approach is again evident, for we are reminded here of Dasein's retaining its actual, past involvements and awaiting potential, future involvements that make possible any relations to the present world. To be engaged in the present, Dasein must be able to refer itself from its retained past to what is awaited as potential; Dasein can be involved because of its general appetition toward regions of possible ready-to-hand experiences. The actual occasion can be involved in—that is, can temporalize and make actual—the extensive continuum because the actual occasion "includes in its own continuities real potentiality which is referent beyond itself" (PR 72).

By this appetitious extensity, contemporary actual occasions belong to a common world, even though they do not prehend each other. Actual occasions, therefore, cannot be simply located, and Whitehead's statement that everything is everywhere becomes even clearer. Contemporaries cohere in an experiential solidarity, for "an act of experience has an objective scheme of extensive order by reason of the . . . fact that its own perspective standpoint has extensive content" (PR 67). The extensive continuum is the expression of this extensive content by which the actual occasion houses not only the past but the present.

Although the actual occasion does not physically prehend the extensive continuum (for it is not actual), the data for the actual occasion's relation to its present world, so to speak, are

the potentialities contributed by contemporary actual occasions to a relational complex. In a similar way, Dasein is always
already within a relational complex of involvements not because of its actual activities but because of the *potentiality* of
the ready-to-hand intentional matrix that *is* Dasein's worldhood. For Whitehead, such potential involvements with the
relational complex of the extensive continuum are perceived
in presentational immediacy. In this mode of perception, "the
contemporary world is consciously prehended" (PR 61). While
causal efficacy provides vague feelings of past occasions and a
dim sense of how such occasions move toward the future,
presentational immediacy "rescues from vagueness a contemporary spatial region" (PR 121). Since the present is not actual,
presentational immediacy is not the perception of contemporary actual occasions but of contemporary *regions* of potentiality that are divisible but not divided into possible atomic
perspectives. In a sense, like presence-at-hand, presentational
immediacy is "barren" (PR 326), for unlike readiness-at-hand,
it offers no sense of the extensive continuum's significance to
the perceiver in terms of past contribution or future relevance.
The function of presentational immediacy is to offer a vivid
portrayal of the present while maintaining the exclusion of
mutual prehensions of contemporary occasions.

## Symbolic Reference

PRESENTATIONAL IMMEDIACY IS the mode of perception that supplies us with a sense of an extensive field for potential becomings. But since there are no actualities that can be perceived in
this field, actual occasions can have no physical prehensions of
the extensive continuum immediately presented. Therefore,
presentational immediacy does not illustrate the actual occasion's subjective involvement with its contemporary, relational
field and so is barren and indifferent toward contemporary
actual occasions (PR 324). However, we know that our experience of the contemporary world is not *about* a mere field.
We experience a present that is populated by animate and

efficacious entities. This experience is made possible by an integration of presentational immediacy and causal efficacy that Whitehead calls "symbolic reference." In this mixed mode of perception, we experience the spatialization of the ecstasis of the present in which a presented locus of extended relations (the content of presentational immediacy) becomes a background for the projection of past appropriations (the content of causal efficacy). For Whitehead, this is our ordinary form of human consciousness.

The content of causal efficacy is tied up with the experience of the witness of the body. These feelings are brought to bear upon the present extended world so that their "pragmatic consequences, involving some future state of bodily feelings" (PR 179) are projected onto the background of the extensive continuum. In this way, "the animal body is the great central ground underlying all symbolic reference" (PR 172). We vaguely feel our "place" in the experiential field by means of causal efficacy, but these indistinct feelings of spatial relations are in need of "localization and discrimination" by presentational immediacy (PR 179). In essence, the sensations of the actual occasion's prehensions are taken to be symbols projected upon the extensive continuum to refer to the becomings of contemporary things in certain spatial regions. The vector character of feelings in causal efficacy allows symbolic reference to disclose present becomings as already felt in the temporal movements of transition. The past is felt as moving into the future, and symbolic reference is the interpolation of the present as symbolized in a region.

Thus, our ordinary conscious experience is, as Kraus writes, a synthesis "of *was* and *could be* into the immediacy of *is.*"[2] Symbolic reference, we might say, is the perceptual mechanism for working out, in Heidegger's terminology, the "as-structures" of the contemporary world. Dasein's state-of-mind and understanding have the dipolar relationship of revealing two equiprimordial aspects of Being-in-the-world: moods reveal *that* Dasein is always in some situation, and understanding interprets *what* the situation may hold. Interpretation discloses what is within the range of immediate possibility by clarifying the as-structures of the worldhood of a particular situation. In its circumspective concern, Dasein understands a tool *as* something to be used for a certain purpose. This "as" is determined by clarifying the involvable "fore-structures."

For example, Dasein is familiar with a certain object as a chair because of what has been retained from previous involvements with chairs and because of potential uses that may be awaited. The formulation of an as-structure occurs on a pre-thematic, prepropositional level of experience by means of three components of fore-structure: ( 1 ) fore-having, Dasein's vague but ever-present understanding of its previous, total involvements with chairs within the matrix of its environment; ( 2 ) fore-sight, Dasein's point of view in a particular situation that allows Dasein to focus its attention upon the chair as a utensil for the purpose of providing a seat; ( 3 ) fore-conception, Dasein's disposition that grasps in advance a definite conception of the chair. Thus, interpretation is a hermeneutic approach to projecting awaited possibilities that is never a presuppositionless possession of given facts.

It is this circle from prior understanding to future, potential involvement that provides the basis for discovering the significance of worldhood. Mehta explains that this

> circle of understanding is not a circle in which some
> arbitrarily chosen mode of knowledge revolves but is
> an expression of the existenzial pre-structure of Dasein
> itself. Far from being vicious, the circle conceals in it-
> self the possibilities of a deeper knowledge . . .
> worked out on the basis of the 'things themselves.'[3]

The hermeneutic, virtuous circle of forestructure makes possible worldly significance and provides for meaning, for *"meaning is the 'upon-which' [das Woraufhin] of a projection in terms of which something becomes intelligible [verstandlich] as something"* (BT 193). Insofar as meaning is connected to Dasein's projection of possibility, Heidegger can state that in a sense, *"only Dasein can be meaningful"* (BT 193). This characterization of meaning, tied to projection, is linked to the ecstatic futurity of existentiality, for as David R. Mason points out,

> Heidegger's use of the term "Whereunto" (Woraufhin) as the equivalent of "meaning" (Sinn) signifies that the entity has a goal beyond itself, but which yet lies at the basis of its Being. This "Whereunto" is such that it makes possible the projection of Dasein, its existing forward.[4]

The relationship of meaning to Dasein's ecstatic, futural projection of potentiality by means of its existentiality does not mean that Dasein can invent possibilities in any manner it wishes. Dasein cannot be and do whatever it likes, for possibility is always limited by actuality. In any given situation, Dasein *may* project meaningful possibilities, but only what it *can* project as meaningful. Edward S. Casey explains:

> In Heidegger's terminology, the "as-structure" here is "existential-hermeneutical," and not apophantic in nature; it expresses an *inherence of the past* in the *present* rather than the reverse; and it does not effect any division into distinct regions of time. The immanence-in-the-present remains operative even when I recognize something *as about to happen*. The "about to" is an intrinsic feature of the recognized object itself.[5]

Again, Dasein's facticity (the actual pole of Being-in-the-world) and existentiality (the potential pole of Being-in-the-world) together "characterize the primordial disclosedness of Being-in-the-world" (BT 188).

Prehensions of past actual occasions provide the fore-structures of regions to be discovered by symbolic reference. Data from these prehensions are projected onto the images of presentational immediacy, which in turn, in an instance of Whitehead's transcendental inquiry, are made possible by the vector movements of causal efficacy. Like the existentially interpretive nature of care, the ecstatic character of concrescence is essentially the hermeneutic activity of appropriation and projection. Symbolic reference is the disclosure of what Heidegger calls *"das Worhaufhin"* (the upon which, where-unto, or destination) of the contemporary world as something that bears relevance or meaning to the actual occasion. Although the actual occasion does not physically prehend its contemporaries, symbolic reference is the mixed mode of perception by which the present world is nevertheless meaningful to the concrescing actual occasion.

The way symbolic reference discloses the meaning of the contemporary world can be seen in the way transmuted physical feelings reveal nexūs. The actual occasion has a multitude of simple physical feelings of many actual occasions. Feelings are discarded so that many in the group are felt to exhibit a certain way of being felt; for instance, they are felt "redly." A corresponding conceptual feeling with the eternal object "red" as its datum is compared and contrasted to all simple physical feelings and therefore "has an impartial relevance to the above-mentioned various simple physical feelings of the various members of the nexus" (PR 250). The complexities involved in transmutation need not be explained here. What is important is that the relevance of the conceptual feeling leads to an integration of all the feelings involved, so that a single, transmuted physical feeling occurs. This "is the way in which the actual world is felt as a community" (PR 251), and it is our "usual way of consciously feeling the world" (PR 253). Sensations are contrasted yet integrated in such a way that they are projected onto a region of extendedness, that is, interpreted as a nexus.

When members of a nexus bear a resemblance so that the group "forms a single line of inheritance of its defining characteristic," it is an "enduring object" (PR 34). Various strands of inheritance within the duration of the nexus may occur, and these variations account for what we experience as change. The temporal identity of the enduring object is achieved through similar patterns of concrescence inherited by actual occasions from past members of the nexus, or members of particular lines of inheritance within the nexus. The temporal continuity of an enduring object, then, is only abstract, for no concrete entity endures through what we perceive as the duration of the nexus. Although each actual occasion in a strand of inheritance sums up the historical route of the strand, what endure and undergo change are shared characteristics in the form of eternal objects that mediate data from past actual occasions to their successors.

Presentational immediacy allows us to interpret the forestructures of the historical route of inheritance occurring in a particular presented locus of the extended continuum. We do not perceive a collection of actual occasions that are parts of a stone as cells are parts of the body. *Stone* properly refers to a contemporary region of extended relations which we take now to be "'grey' on the assumption that this contemporary region is the prolongation, of that historic route, into the presented locus" (PR 172). The physical feelings contributing to causal efficacy are transmuted into a feeling of the objectified nexus that we call a stone. The complex interplay between causal efficacy and presentational immediacy involved in symbolic reference provides a perception not of an objectified stone in the present but an image projected onto a region that symbolizes the progressive continuity of a historical route of inheritance. Causal efficacy is the appropriation of vectors: what is felt there is felt here. Symbolic reference is the way a presented locus, perceived in presentational immediacy, becomes the place of the destination *(das Woraufhin)* of vectors: what is here is felt there.

Provided by symbolic reference with a perception of (though no physical prehension of) its contemporaries, the concrescing actual occasion has an image of its present community. The actual occasion and its contemporaries in the stone are involved in "a unison of becoming,' constituting a positive relation of all the occasions in this community to any one of them" (PR 124). While contemporaries do not physically prehend one another, they stand in "mutual relatedness" by which they are in "concrescent unison" (PR 124). Belonging to a particular locus of mutual relatedness is taken into account in an actual occasion's concrescence.

The concrescent unison of contemporary actual occasions may be compared with Heidegger's notion of destiny. Dasein's historicality, the fateful projection of its heritage, is tied up with the broader historicality of Dasein's generation as historically Being-with-Others. The destiny of the actual occasion is wrapped up in its concrescent unison with others and the "social background, of which it is a part" (PR 90). Although the presented locus of presentational immediacy itself refers to neither the past nor the future, symbolic reference reflects the historical relations between contemporaries "as forming a background in layers of social order, the defining characteristic becoming wider and more general as we widen the background" (PR 90).

## *Spatiality*

THE SPATIAL FEATURES OF THE actual occasion's experience are now becoming clearer, and for Heidegger, "Dasein itself is 'spatial' with regard to its Being-in-the-world" (BT 138)— space belongs to Dasein. Perhaps this is best illustrated by an aspect of Dasein's spatiality termed "directionality" *(Ausrichtung)*. Dasein directs utensils to their proper "regions" *(Gegenden)* of handiness to display best their in-order-to. In a workshop, a hammer is near other instruments of carpentry not only in the ordinary sense of *near* but also in the sense that it is placed in a way that facilitates Dasein's use of the hammer. Dasein "makes room" for the hammer in its regional relations to certain other tools as distinct from others. Even when physically touching a fork, the hammer is "nearer" a nail that may be yards away. This nearness is due to the significance that Dasein assigns to hammers-and-nails but not to hammers-and-forks. Space appears in Dasein's placings of mallets-and-chisels, needles-and-thread, shovels-and-picks.

Hand in hand with directionality goes "de-severance" *(Entferung)*. "*In Dasein there lies an essential tendency towards closeness*" (BT 140) whereby the feet-and-inches "distances of Things present-at-hand do not coincide with the remoteness and closeness of what is ready-to-hand" (BT 141). The earth beneath the carpenter's feet is certainly closer in the ordinary sense than the hammer he approaches. But a measurement of this sort is an abstraction of sorts, for the earth and hammer are considered out of the context of the carpenter's involvemental project and therefore are viewed as present-at-hand.

While his point is that space is best understood to reveal the worldhood of the world when considered in terms of Dasein's comportment with the ready-to-hand, Heidegger admits a certain unavoidable subjectivist sound to this treatment of spatiality and remarks that

> this 'subjectivity' perhaps uncovers the 'Reality' of the world at its most Real; it has nothing to do with 'subjective' arbitrariness or subjectivist 'ways of taking' an entity which 'in itself' is otherwise. *The circumspective de-severing of Dasein . . . reveals the Being-in-itself of the 'true world'.* (BT 141)

This passage represents an important theme for Heidegger. In making metaphysical claims about reality, philosophers have typically considered objects apart from the way we exist alongside them in the world; that is, reality is usually treated as present-at-hand. While presence-at-hand is one mode of the Being of things. Heidegger insists that Dasein's absorption in readiness-to-hand is primordial. Because Dasein's first and foremost relationship to its world (its "true world," above) is involvemental, the existential analytic requires that readiness-to-hand take precedence. Readiness-to-hand is the subject of an ontology of the concrete, meaningful world, and presence-at-hand yields a categorial scheme of a collection of abstractions.

Heidegger briefly discusses the way space is disclosed by means of Dasein's temporality. Showing that "Dasein's spatiality is 'embraced by temporality'" is not an exercise in "deducing space from time," and Heidegger's aim "is also different from the priority of time over space in Kant's sense" (BT 418). To say that Dasein is spatial is to say that

> Dasein takes in space; this is to be understood literally. It is by no means just present-at-hand in a bit of space which its body fills up. In existing, it has already made room for its own leeway. . . . Nor does the distinction between the 'spatiality' of an extended Thing

and that of Dasein lie in the fact that Dasein *knows* about space; for taking space in [das Raum-einnehmen] is so far from identical with a 'representing' of the spatial, that it is presupposed by it instead. (BT 419)

Heidegger emphasizes that an account of spatiality, as with any other existential structure, cannot be reduced to epistemology. Rather, spatiality is the way Dasein "breaks into space" (BT 421) in the de-severance of equipment. Dasein's leeway consists in directing tools to their places in a region. Retaining its involvements, Dasein awaits a region that opens up *when* a tool is used:

> With regard to that space which [Dasein] has ecstatically taken in, the "here" of its current factical situation [Lage bzw. Situation] never signifies a position in space, but signifies rather the leeway of the range of that equipmental totality with which it is most closely connected—a leeway which has opened up for it in directionality and de-severance. (BT 420)

It is important to note that regions open up in current situations, for this indicates that space is primarily associated with the present. Although Heidegger insists upon "the 'coupling together' of space and time" (BT 420), he recognizes that the presencing of a region provides the basis for our language to be "dominated through and through with 'spatial representations'" that lead us to speak as if space and time occurred separately (BT 421). The important point here is that Dasein's temporality, which makes it possible to await and retain involvemental encounters, enables Dasein's spatial experience of the world.

For Heidegger, regions represent the way things are "placed" in relation to a matrix of relations. A certain parallel is found here in Whitehead. Actual occasions are felt not just singly but as occupying places within the extensive continuum. The places are arranged according to the relations holding among groups of actual occasions forming a nexus. The retaining and awaiting that make possible Dasein's ready-to-hand involvements also make possible the placing of things in keeping with those ready-to-hand involvements. As we have seen, retaining and awaiting are made possible by ecstatic temporality. For Whitehead, the actual occasion feels not just sensations but also, by symbolic reference, sensations of a "stone" as a regional unity (nexus). While the individual sensations are appropriated from the past, they are projected onto the present region.

Whitehead conceives of a region as a locus of extended relations and therefore as a certain kind of nexus. The region I perceive before me is populated by a number of nexūs (a pen, a sheet of paper, a lamp, etc.) that stand in those extended relations presentationally immediate in my perception. At the same time, the nexus that is my body also bears extended relations to the other things in this region. But my spatiality is not due to the existentiell relations that I bear in various, particular regions, for "concrescence presupposes its basic region, and not the region its concrescence" (PR 283). The actual occasion is essentially extensive, both temporally and spatially. To occur in a particular spatial standpoint is a necessary condition of any experience an actual occasion may have, just as experiences occur within particular, temporal perspectives. An experience cannot be understood apart from its spatiotemporal situation. But the spatiotemporal situation of the experiencer can be understood only because the experiencer is the sort of entity that happens temporally and spatially extensively. This transcendental analysis of spatial experience is evident in the following passage in which Whitehead writes that in his

> general description of the state of extension, nothing
> has been said about physical time or physical space, or
> of the more general notion of creative advance. These
> are notions which presuppose the more general relationship of extension. They express additional facts
> about the actual occasions. The extension of space is
> really the spatialization of extension; and the extension
> of time is really the temporalization of extension. (PR
> 288-89)

For Heidegger, a spatial situation is the way Dasein makes a place for itself by making places for potential involvements with the ready-to-hand. These placings bring about a matrix of regions in present, extended relations. Similarly for Whitehead, the actual occasion's extended relation within the extensive continuum involves a matrix of subregions and intermediate regions (PR 287–88). In its essential extendedness, the intentionality of the actual occasion provides a "general scheme of relationships providing the capacity that many objects can be welded into the real unity of one experience" (PR 67). This matrix can be experienced as a unity because it is only potentially divisible. Since contemporary actual occasions, although atomic, are not physically prehended, and since an image of a spatial region is of the present, the "objectification of the contemporary world merely expresses that world in terms of its potentiality for subdivision and in terms of the mutual perspectives which any subdivision will bring into real effectiveness" (PR 67).

The actual occasion experiences this matrix as a potentially divisible quantum in the same way that the phases of concrescence are only potentially divisible (PR 284). The satisfied actual occasion may be divided in its prehensions by a succeeding actual occasion that positively prehends only certain elements in the previous actual occasion. The past actual occasion is given not just as an historical summary of its past world in a temporal quantum but also as an extended actuality expressing spatial relations. Prehended actual occasions, then, have extensive content and are "objectified with the retention of their extensive relations" (PR 67). But in the experience of the concrescing actual occasion, its own spatial situation is a potentially divisible matrix of extended relations. Space is the spatial potential of actual occasions.

Each actual occasion expresses the extended relations of its own spatial standpoint, and the regions expressed by these standpoints are experienced as interconnected. But what can be described phenomenologically about the content of the experiences of this interconnectedness? In other words, what is the content of an experience of a spatial relation? Whitehead answers first by offering a transcendental analysis of the possibility of spatial unity by describing the geometric relation within a nexus and then by explaining that the actual occasion spatializes its world by means of its physical feelings of those geometric relations.

Whitehead develops a complex, formal, metageometrical explanation of spatial connections; a detailed account need not be attempted here. What is important is that the actual occasions within a focal region are spatially related in terms of Whitehead's special sense of straight lines (and "flat loci"). These straight lines and other structures in this metageometry are not just formal features of an abstract mathematics—they are spatial structures experienced by actual occasions. A physical prehension of a straight line is called a "strain." Strains are not separate feelings, though; they are felt along with physical feelings of the appropriations of the past. By the vector character of feelings, what is there is felt here. By the strain-feelings that are part of these vector feelings, what is there is felt as coming from some particular *direction* relative to the spatial standpoint of the experiencer.

The experiencer's standpoint is a "seat" of intersecting lines. The straight lines felt in strains delineate "a region of dense concurrence of straight lines defined by the 'seat'" (PR 312). Although the lines that define these regions are structures already (potentially) in the extensive continuum, the perception of a region by an actual occasion actualizes and projects these structures onto a presented locus. Through strain feelings, the actual occasion "lifts into importance the complete lines, planes, and three-dimensional flats, which are defined by the seat of the strain" (PR 310).

The sensations of causal efficacy involve strains that along with the sensa of the prehensions associated with the perception of causal efficacy, contribute to the data of transmutation. Identifying a nexus through transmutation, symbolic reference produces experience of a region of the extensive continuum defined by straight lines and a seat of those lines that is the perspectival standpoint of the experiencer. Presentational immediacy tells us that the region is presently before us, and causal efficacy tells us that the past occasions (forming the historical route of the current nexus) were felt in certain spatial relations. By symbolic reference, the experiencer has an image of the contemporary world that exhibits those relations. Kraus illustrates this event:

> Just as the geometry already inherent in a scene-to-be-painted is transformed from the standpoint of the painter's eye into the geometry which appears on the canvas, so each actual occasion performs its section of an already geometrized actual world via its strain feelings of that world from its perspectival standpoint. It actualizes a strain in the physical world; it introduces a perspectival geometry of the world from its vantage point and publicly bequeaths it to the future.[6]

The "common ground" between presentational immediacy and causal efficacy in this process is found in the presented locus and eternal objects (PR 168). The historical routes of inherited strain-feelings provide the perceptual region for a nexus in presentational immediacy. When we look at a stone, presentational immediacy gives a sense of a focal region by means of eye-strain (PR 170). This focal region is correlated to sensa inherited in causal efficacy by feelings of bodily efficacy in the eyes. What become integrated are "(i) the causal efficacy of the antecedent eye in the vision, (ii) the presentational immediacy of the stone-image, (iii) the presentational immediacy of the eye-strain" (PR 173). This is what we *mean* in saying that we see the stone *with* our eyes. At the same time, the eternal objects that color prehensions are assumed, because of the vector feelings in causal efficacy, to continue into the present. By projecting the eternal object by which the eye feels "grayly" onto the presented locus, causal efficacy and presentational immediacy are integrated in symbolic reference.

While strain feelings are particularly relevant to our ordinary conscious experience, Whitehead's phenomenology of spatiality emphasizes the important point that strains are felt in the body. The initial strain-feeling involved in causal efficacy has its seat in a bodily organ—for instance, the hand. As the geometrized focal region becomes integrated with the feeling of the hand-strain, the sense of the withness of the body is retained as the eternal object, say, of the "roundly" felt stone, is projected onto the presented locus. The withness of the body in symbolic reference "is the feeling of the sense-datum as generally implicated in the whole region (of antecedent 'seats' and focal regions) geometrically defined by the inherited strains" (PR 313). In this sense, presentational immediacy is derived from causal efficacy as "strands of transmission of bodily efficacy . . . converge upon the same focal region as picked out by the many bodily 'strains'" (PR 313). Thus, causal efficacy "is more primitive than the feeling of presentational immediacy that issues from it" (PR 312), for the feelings of "geometrical strain in the body . . . govern the whole process of presentational immediacy" (PR 126; see also PR 333).

Like Heidegger, Whitehead presents a transcendental investigation into the possibility of spatial experience that shows that a theoretical, abstract account of space is derivative from the primary spatiality of the actual occasion. Spatiality is the way the actual occasion, like Dasein, "breaks into space" (BT 421). Regions open up in Dasein's current situation; so space is primarily associated with Dasein's present. Something similar is true in the situation of the actual occasion, for space is represented in the geometric relations of the *presented* locus. But the opening up of space is due to Dasein's retaining and awaiting, and the experience of the presented locus is due to the actual occasion's strain feelings found in appropriations of the past that can be projected by means of their vector movements.

For both Whitehead and Heidegger, then, there is a temporal basis for spatiality. Only by means of the temporal movements of vectors through an entity that can appropriate and project feelings of those vectors can a scientific account of space be possible. Strain-feelings form the basis for geometrizing the experienceable world, but these feelings are projected upon a present, potential region and are "irrespective of the actualities which constitute the environment" (PR 326). By symbolically referring to a presented locus, strain-feelings are the actual occasion's expressions of potentialities of extension, so "scientific measurements merely concern the systematic real potentiality out of which actualities arise" (PR 326). Thus, Whitehead offers not only an account of the experiencer's spatiality that parallels Heidegger's in important ways but also a view of the theory-praxis relation that is similar to Heidegger's: we can study the world as thematizing observers only because we experience the world primordially as involved Being-in-the-world.

# 7

# *The Experience of the Holy*

H EIDEGGER'S AND WHITEHEAD'S transcendental inquiries into human experience disclose the spatiotemporal structures that make our experience possible. Although both philosophers show that these structures provide unity to the experiencer's existence, the concept of authenticity in *Being and Time* makes it clear that Heidegger is more concerned than Whitehead with a need to unite our fragmented everyday existence.[1] However, what I wish to show at this point is that the work of both thinkers can be used to provide an interpretation of certain special experiences that bring about a unity of our ordinary spatially and temporally heterogeneous experiences in such a way that a wholeness of our existence is illuminated. I shall call these special experiences *holy* and our everyday, diverse experiences *profane*. I suggest this description of holy experience as a way of making possible a coherence of life. In this way, perhaps, our transcendental inquiry reaches consummation.

My use of the term *holy* need not be construed in its traditionally religious sense. We all recognize that certain phaces hold a special power to evoke intensely personal feelings: one's birthplace, a loved one's grave, or a national monument. But we find that our normal, spatial experience of the world is fragmented. We live in a heterogeny of places. We eat in certain places, sleep in others, and work in others. Although some activities may take place in a number of places, most places are appropriate for some things but not others. For example, it may not be appropriate to dance where it is appropriate to view works of art. Singing is out of place where serious discussion is fitting. Some places, perhaps vacant lots, may seem appropriate for nothing in particular or even nothing at all. In some places we feel at home, in others uncomfortably foreign. Perhaps the only true relationship among all the various places we encounter in our everyday existence is sheer diversity.

The same may be said for our normal, temporal experience. We all recognize the special power of certain times or events: a wedding or a funeral. But our normal experience contains times for work, times for sleep, times for eating, good and bad times, easy and hard times. Thus, there is unrelatedness regarding our multiplicity of profane involvements. We find a fixed point neither in time nor in space in our ordinary experience of the world to be the source that unifies our fragmented existence to allow a wholeness of self.[2]

We live through our unrelated everyday experiences by means of routine. But the experiences that I call holy stand out from the routine. They are set apart, special, extraordinary. A funeral or a wedding possesses some unique power to produce reverence, and we recognize these things to be of great importance and urgency, not to be taken lightly, inspiring and often celebratory. These holy things in some way exemplify a "life-and-death"[3] character that points to the entirety of one's existence. At the same time, these holy experiences appear as things that are not-to-be-disgraced. Not to dis-grace the holy experience is not to dis-favor or un-gift it. This gift character of the holy is disclosed when we view such experiences as life-and-death situations from which we receive a sense of wholeness, of connectedness of our lives.

Just as authenticity for Heidegger is not something that floats above everydayness, the ability of the holy to unify our ordinary experiences is due to the fact that the holy is not disconnected from the profane. In *The Idea of the Holy,* Rudolf Otto describes the "numinous" as the quality of holy experience that sets it apart from what is rationally schematizable, so that this numinous feature is "a unique, original feeling-response" that is irreducible to any other experience.[4] Otto's book is illuminating in many ways, but in striving to divorce his treatment of the holy from considerations of morality, he ultimately overemphasizes the otherness of numinous experience.

John A. T. Robinson, discussing Christian worship in *Honest to God,* keeps the deep connection between the holy and the profane more clearly in view when he writes that "the holy is the 'depth' of the common, just as the 'secular' is not a (godless) section of life but the world . . . cut off from its true depth."[5] One who experiences the holy wishes to integrate it with the everyday world by letting this depth give meaning to one's life. Robinson illustrates the connection of the holy to the profane in an example concerning the Christian ceremony of Holy Communion:

> The bread and the wine that stand at the heart of the action and form its basis are samples only of all other common things and the focus of all other common relationships. The Holy Communion is the proclamation to the Church and to the world that the presence of Christ with his people is tied to a right receiving of the common. . . . It must be made to represent the truth that the 'beyond' is to be found 'at the centre of life.'[6]

Although this passage reminds us again of Heidegger's insistence that authenticity must occur amid average everydayness, the connection with the profane is not enough to make the holy understood in the same way we understand our ordinary involvements. An essential feature of the holy is precisely the fact that the holy appears as unthematizable and mysterious. Paul Tillich writes that in the holy there "is a presence which remains mysterious in spite of its appearance, and it exercizes both an attractive and a repulsive function in those who encounter it."[7] Otto makes much of this dual character of *mysterium tremendum* and *fascinans:*

These two qualities, the daunting and the fascinating, now combine in strange harmony of contrasts, . . . at once the strangest and most noteworthy phenomenon in the whole history of religion. The daemonic-divine object may appear to the mind an object of horror and dread, but at the same time it is no less something that allures with a potent charm, and the creature, who trembles before it, utterly cowed and cut down, has always at the same time the impulse to turn to it, nay even make it his own.[8]

We encounter the holy in a state of reverence, at times to the point of fear, yet we are attracted to this mysterious power and wish to embrace it as our own. The holy appears in its awful otherness, and it is this quality (upon which Otto focuses) that we find attractive even as we are repelled. The holy is something I wish to take up and somehow make part of me, and in doing so, I necessarily take it to my profane existence. Ernst Cassirer finds the twofold character of holy (or sacred) experience to parallel the sacred-profane polarity. In the holy experience, writes Cassirer,

mere bestial terror becomes astonishment moving in a twofold direction, composed of opposite emotions— fear and hope, awe and admiration. . . . For the sacred always appears *at once* as the distant and the near, as the familiar and protective but at the same time as the absolutely inaccessible. . . . The consequence of this two-fold character is that in differentiating itself from empirical, profane substance, the sacred does not simply *repel* it but progressively *permeates* it; in its opposition it still retains the ability to give form to its opposite.[9]

Thus, although the holy reveals itself as mysterious—that is, reveals itself (as Heidegger says of Being) as unwilling to reveal itself completely and thereby cannot be understood in the same way that we understand ordinary, profane things—this very unwillingness connects the holy to the profane. We are reminded of Heidegger's description of the call of conscience that comes in the threatening experience of anxiety. In spite of the uncanniness associated with the experience, the receiver of the call recognizes that conscience points to the ability to experience a wholeness of self, a unity that the receiver of the call wants to have. Like the call of conscience from whose otherness we are repelled and for whose extraordinariness we have anxiety, we are nevertheless attracted to the mystery of the holy and believe that it somehow gives form to the profane.

The deep connection between the holy and the profane offers insight into the peculiar spatiality of the holy. Hans-Georg Gadamer points out that the "'profane' is the *place in front of* the sanctuary. . . . [And] the profane has remained a concept related to the *area* of the sacred and determined by it alone." [10] For Gadamer, the relationship between the holy and the profane is primarily spatial: the profane is literally outside of the holy; a reference to the *place* of the holy is what locates the profane. The profane world is a heterogeneity of places, but spatial homogeneity can be established in an experience of holy place. Cassirer writes that the boundaries set up for a holy place "are the starting point from which begins the setting of boundaries in space and from which, and by a progressive process of organization and articulation, the process spreads over the whole of the physical cosmos." [11]

Understanding the holy as *here* and the profane as *there*—and *there* and *there*—reveals the peculiar way holy space transcends profane space. By the spatial boundaries of the holy, one is able to bound the profane. Distinct profane places are related together by the centrality of the holy place. The holy place is experienced as the center of one's worldhood. In the holy place, I am at the source of placing. In this way, the holy place has the ecstatic power to point beyond itself to the rest of one's possible places to occupy. We are aware in the holy experience "of systematic elements in the extensive relationship between the seat of the immediate feeler and the region concerned" (PR 314). More important, this experience of holy place illuminates what Whitehead calls "'projected' sensations, involving regions of contemporary space beyond the body" (PR 314) as well as regions that lie outside the particular holy region.

For instance, the churchgoer views what is outside the church as meaningless unless somehow related to the church. The church is experienced as the center of all possible places to inhabit, the focal point of all that is outside. As the central place of religious life, the church exemplifies the Latin root *religare,* "to bind back." Thus, the churchgoer's heterogeneous profane places in which the churchgoer finds himself are made homogeneous by being bound back to their religious focus. Similarly, the sanctity of one's birthplace can provide a focus for profane places when experienced as the source of one's placeability. It is the place that makes possible other places. Standing in this place of my source, I view my possible placings as conditioned by the facticity of my *original* place.

The place of one's wedding also reveals this capacity to make the heterogeneous homogeneous. The marriage ceremony is one that proclaims a new source of one's self *with another.* The ceremony is a consecration of Being-with-one-another in which we may say that the couple's lives are "determined by the manner in which their Dasein, each in its own way, has been taken hold of" (BT 159). The wedding place is the site at which the couple proclaims that they intend to be *"authentically* bound together, and this makes possible the right kind of objectivity [die rechte Sachlichkeit], which frees the Other in his freedom for himself" (BT 159). The marriage place is a point of renewal of all of one's places; it is a place where the presence of the spouse enters all of one's possible placings.

These examples show that a holy place has the power to move outside itself to unify the unrelated places of one's profane existence. Losing ourselves amid the scattered places of routine, our everyday existence, says Heidegger, is basically one of distractions. The profane tendency to scurry care-less-ly from one thing to another, says Heidegger, leads to the mode of existence in which Dasein "entangles itself in itself, so that

the distracted not-tarrying becomes *never-dwelling-anywhere*.
. . . In never dwelling anywhere, Being-there is everywhere
and nowhere" (BT 398). In this passage, Heidegger is concerned with the temporality of everydayness, but it is important
to note that his description of distraction is written in spatial
language, and it shows the need to be authentically situated.
This lack of situatedness, the absence of focus and situatedness,
is the essence of profane existence. Our everyday experiences
become placed centrally by the consecration of holy place.

The consecration of a holy place brings us directly to the
discussion of the temporal aspects of the holy. The time of the
holy place is manifest in a manner different from that of a profane place. Heidegger writes that a Greek temple "first fits together and at the same time gathers around itself the unity of
those paths and relations in which birth and death . . . acquire the shape of destiny for human being." [12] The unifying
principle in which the temple gathers up all that is around it is
tied directly to birth and death—the unique temporal structure in that the holy manifests itself as a life-and-death situation.
For Whitehead, the actual occasion can be fully understood
only in its concrete process of concrescence. This internal
process includes the whole of its becoming; the actual occasion is at once a summation of its history and the anticipation
of its satisfaction. The holy experience is what illuminates this
dynamic temporality.

The wholeness of temporality is especially evident at the
grave of a loved one. While a grave is typically (and, of course,
correctly) considered a place, its holiness cannot be abstracted
from the fact that it memorializes the temporal end of another.
Since it is the end of *all* (but the memory) of the loved one,
we are forced to consider the loved one in his or her *entirety*.
For Whitehead, a living person is in some way a nexus of occasions that supports "a thread of personal order along some
historic route of its members" (PR 107). The temporal power
of the experience of the grave is its ability to call attention to
that unifying historical route that gathers together one's diverse, profane experiences. So not only is the temporal struc-

ture of the holy an essential factor in holy places, but this example reveals something of the holy's nature of unifying a life-*time* of experiences.

The holy event (which may not be essentially related to a particular holy place) can be seen to create a unity of the profane by means of its cyclical, renewing nature. Whitehead writes that the world

> craves for novelty and yet is haunted by terror at the loss of the past, with its familiarities and its loved ones. It seeks escape from time in its character of 'perpetually perishing.' Part of the joy of the new years is the hope of the old round seasons, with their stable facts—of friendship, and love, and old association. (PR 340)

Our means of overcoming the loss of the perpetually perishing world is to unify what is lost with what is present by ceremonial renewal. The notion of a temporal cycle is especially evident in such ceremonies as harvest celebrations. The harvest is viewed as a holy time that returns and renews itself each year, as we are renewed by the nourishment of the harvested crops. In the process, all that happens in between is unified.

The harvest itself, however, is not lost, for it returns each year. But events such as birth, death, and reaching adulthood (not a particular event yet still more or less a particular time period of one's life) happen only once. It is precisely the fact that these events happen only once that requires we must renew them. This is most clear in the events of birth and death. Birth is a holy event that focuses upon one end of its life-and-death character, for I celebrate my birth as the source of my entire life. By affirming my source in a birthday celebration, I reestablish not just my birth but the *whole* of my life. In renewing the whole of my life, in recognizing how my historicality stretches me along from birth to death, I give unity to the fragmented, profane world that involves the greatest portion of my time. A funeral emphasizes the other end of the life-and-death nature of the holy, and it too is a remembrance and a renewal of the whole of one's existence. Finally, the recognition of achieving adulthood is a onetime occurrence, and it is seen as a new source. At the time of reaching adulthood, I am reborn and view my life as a whole, for I do not consider only what lies ahead in my future but also re-view all that has gone before, sacred and profane. My life in the world is being regenerated and at the same time unified.

The cyclical and renewing nature of these holy events disclose the ecstatic temporality of our experiences of them. While profane events are simply events *in* life, as John E. Smith writes, holy events are events *of* life.[13] Holy events can be understood in the New Testament sense of *kairos,* a time of fulfillment in which the temporal horizons of these experiences point beyond themselves to include the whole of one's time. For Whitehead and Heidegger, the whole of one's time extends beyond even the concrete events of birth and death. A good example is a memorial to one's forebears. In the holy place dedicated to the founders of my country or ancestors or war heroes, I encounter as part of my source events that took place long before my concrete origin of birth. A holy encounter in which I take up and reappropriate my forebearers as source is much like what Heidegger calls taking over one's "heritage," in which there is "a *handing down* to oneself of the possibilities that have come down to one" (BT 435). In this repetition of "going back into the possibilities of Dasein that has-been-here" (BT 437), I renew the past in my present. Whitehead says that the "man-at-one-moment concentrates in himself the colour of his past,"[14] and we recall that for Whitehead, one's past extends back indefinitely.

At the same time, the holy experience allows me to transcend my concrete future potentiality in viewing the whole of my existence. The point of establishing the holy place of a memorial is that it *will be* renewed again and again. While we may agree with Whitehead that all occasions pass into objective immortality, there are certain events whose objective immortality is especially celebrated or whose tragedy we especially wish to be remembered. We wish to call attention to our demand that "the insistent craving that zest for existence be refreshed by the ever-present, unfading importance of our immediate actions, which perish and yet live for evermore" (PR 351).

Along with their ecstatic temporal and spatial structures, some holy events present themselves as holy-with-others. A marriage necessarily involves another, and a couple celebrates a wedding anniversary as a co-memoration of each other as new source for one another. All of one's profane activities can be seen as relating to one's new-source-in-another, so those profane activities are focused toward the renewal of the wedding ceremony. For many religious persons, a church service necessarily involves a congregation. This holy-with-others event is then seen as giving form to one's life *as* part of the living body of the church. Like Heidegger's concept of destiny as cohistorizing with Others and Whitehead's notion of the unison of becoming of contemporaries, the holy experience sometimes provides wholeness only as wholeness-with-others. We become removed from our routine sense of public time in these holy events to experience a wholeness-with-others not found in the fragmentary world of distraction.

This wholeness of one's existence is the very reason why some events are revealed as holy for others and not holy for me. My holy experiences reveal *my* source and *my* wholeness, and as Whitehead says, "My process of 'being myself' is my origination from my possession of the world" (PR 81). An event that does not illuminate my appropriation of the world into my being does not cause *mysterium tremendum* and *fascinans* in me. I recognize and respect a Hindu ritual as holy-for-*them*. A Chinese commemoration of an ancient hero is an event that does not speak to me as my source, does not create the fascination that my life can be unified, does not bring about the anxiety that my life and death are called into question. Like the call of conscience, a holy event must reveal a summons that "comes *from* me and yet *from beyond me and over me*" (BT 320). The summons comes "from me" in that it is my life that is called into question in the holy experience;

yet the summons comes from "beyond me and over me" in that it is not profane, ordinary, everyday.

There are a few further aspects of the holy experience that I wish to consider. What is revealed about the temporal and spatial structures of our involvement with a holy object that is in our normal manner of speaking neither a place nor an event? In the case of a book of holy scripture, for instance, appropriate times and places are revealing. It seems inappropriate to religious to read scripture *during* a profane activity—say, during a ball game or while watching a movie. It is important to the reader of the scripture that the encounter with the text be set apart from profane encounters. Similarly, certain places are appropriate for reading scripture, such as a church or a particular area of the home that is set aside for reverent activity. Also, can there be a holy place without holy time or a holy time without holy place? I do not wish to suggest that the spatial and temporal aspects of *anything* are properly separable, just as the shape and color of an object are separable only in abstraction. To ask whether there can be a holy place without holy time, then, is an ill-formed question. The ecstatically spatial structure of a holy place is recognized as holy *while* encountered, and during an encounter with a holy place, its temporal aspects are revealed. Similarly, we understand what a Christian means in complaining that he or she wishes to be in church (or maybe at home) during the holy time of Christmas.

My claim has not been that holy experiences are the only means of focusing or unifying our existence. There may be numerous activities, exercises, or even neurotic behaviors that in some sense provide a focus for one's life. My claim is only that we have certain experiences that illuminate our ecstatic temporality and spatiality and that through these special experiences we relate to the world in a manner that calls forth our spatiotemporal wholeness. Whitehead writes that "the essence of an organism is that it is one thing which functions and is spread through space. Now functioning takes time. Thus a biological organism is a unity with a spatiotemporal extension which is the essence of its being."[15] The holy experience reveals that this spatiotemporal extension extends beyond the temporal horizons of birth and death as a unified gathering of events and outward past the horizons of our particular spatial situations to homogenize our possible placings. The life-and-death character of the holy provides us with an understanding of our entire life cycle, as a whole. What is ordinarily fragmented is fully understood when extraordinarily unified.

# Conclusion

> Thus the task of philosophy is to penetrate beyond the
> more obvious accidents to those principles of exis-
> tence which are presupposed in dim consciousness,
> as involved in the total meaning of seeming clarity.
> Philosophy asks the simple question, "What is it all
> about?" In human experience, the philosophic ques-
> tion can receive no final answer. Human knowledge is
> a process of approximation. In the focus of experience
> there is comparative clarity. But the discrimination of
> this clarity leads into the penumbral background. . . .
> The problem is to discriminate exactly what we know
> vaguely.[1]

Whitehead expresses here the broadest conviction underlying both *Process and Reality* and *Being and Time.* There is
much that we know vaguely and through which we involve
ourselves in worldly experience. But we are usually so dimly
conscious of this penumbral background that we mistake the
more clearly present aspects of our experiences as explanatory
of what in fact makes possible any clarity. Content to sail in
circles upon the bright surface, we miss the dark wonders of
the depth.

Heidegger provides an existential phenomenology that allows us to investigate the undercurrents that keep our surface
experiences afloat. We can have particular experiences only
because we exist openly toward a world with which we be-

come involved. We literally care about the world, and although we can sometimes step back from our intimate engagements with the components of the world to consider those things apart from our relations to them, even this abstractive activity is possible only because those are things to which we are primordially, care-ful-ly attached. In the examination of those care-ful attachments, Heidegger shows that our openness toward them comes from our ecstatic temporality by which we take up our past and project it into our future.

Heidegger's notion of our experiential openness has its analogue in Whitehead's view that "events are the relata of the fundamental homogeneous relation of 'extension.'"[2] The actual occasion openly extends toward its past to appropriate its past and to aim these appropriations toward its future. In this way, "every event extends over other events which are part of itself, and every event is extended over by other events of which it is a part."[3] The actual occasion is Being-in-the-world, an event that self-creates and self-interprets through its involvement with the other events in its world.

What I have attempted to show is that both philosophers seek to disclose by means of transcendental inquiry the existential structures that make experiential openness possible. It is clear that for Heidegger, the paradigmatic case for this inquiry is the human experiencer. By following Heidegger's lead, I have tried to show that Whitehead's work can be seen in much the same way. When we inquire into what we vaguely know about the way we feel the world moving through us, in our feelings of causal efficacy, for instance, we are able to discriminate the structures that make experience intelligible.

"Of course," writes Whitehead, "anybody who has any sense who writes on philosophy knows, or ought to know, that the world is unfathomable in its complexity."[4] At best, I have drawn an outline of a transcendental inquiry into the possibility of experience by using the work of two great thinkers. There is much more that can be said about our polymorphous experiences. The chapter on holy experience is an attempt to show how this study can be verified in and applied to particular sorts of experience. But as Heidegger insists, such a philosophical analysis is always a hermeneutic one: the spiral closes in on its center but never finally completes itself. The works of Whitehead and Heidegger greatly tighten the spin of the inquiry's path in clarifying the vague.

CHAPTER ONE

1. Alfred North Whitehead, *Process and Reality: An Essay in Cosmology,* corrected ed., ed. David Ray Griffin and Donald W. Sherburne (New York: Free Press, 1978). Martin Heidegger, *Being and Time,* trans. John Macquarrie and Edward Robinson (New York: Harper and Row, 1962). Further references to these texts will be indicated by PR for *Process and Reality* and BT for *Being and Time* with page numbers.

2. Calvin O. Shrag, "Whitehead and Heidegger: Process Philosophy and Existential Philosophy," *Dialectica* 13 (March 1959): 42–56. The most notable exception to this lack of comparison is David R. Mason's *Time and Providence: An Essay Based on an Analysis of the Concept of Time in Whitehead and Heidegger* (Washington, DC: University Press of America, 1982). In *Insights and Oversights of Great Philosophers* (Albany: State University of New York Press, 1983) and his review of *Being and Time,* in *The Philosophical Review* 38 (1929): 284–91, Charles Hartshorne makes a number of brief comparisons of the two thinkers. Other brief passages comparing process thought with phenomenology are found in Herbert Spiegelberg's *The Phenomenological Movement: A Historical Introduction* (The Hague: Martinus Nijhoff, 1965), vol. 1, pp. 78–79, and vol. 2, p. 525; Marjorie Grene, *The Knower and the Known* (Berkeley: University of California Press, 1974), pp. 244–45, 251. Also, some phenomenologists influenced by Heidegger make some reference to Whitehead, such as Edward S. Casey in *Remembering: A Phenomenological Study* (Bloomington: Indiana University Press, 1987).

3. Alfred North Whitehead, *Modes of Thought* (New York: G. P. Putnam's Sons, 1958), p. 67.

4. Whitehead, *The Interpretation of Science: Selected Essays,* ed. A. H. Johnson (New York: Bobbs Merrill, 1961), p. 205.

5. Calvin O. Schrag, *Existence and Freedom: Towards an Ontology of Human Finitude* (Evanston, IL.: Northwestern University Press, 1970), p. 10.

6. Schrag, *Existence and Freedom,* p. 12.

7. Whitehead, *Modes of Thought,* p. 158.

8. Alfred North Whitehead, *Adventures of Ideas* (New York: Macmillan, 1933; rep., New York: Free Press, 1967), p. 176; my stress.

9. Hubert L. Dreyfus and Stuart E. Dreyfus, "Making a Mind Versus Modeling the Brain," *Daedalus* (Winter 1988): 24–25.

10. Elizabeth M. Kraus, *The Metaphysics of Experience: A Companion to Whitehead's "Process and Reality"* (New York: Fordham University Press, 1979), pp. 41–42.

11. Cf. Michael E. Zimmerman, *Eclipse of the Self: The Development of Heidegger's Concept of Authenticity* (Athens: Ohio University Press, 1981), p. 35.

12. Theodore Kisiel, "Towards a Topology of Dasein," in *Heidegger: The Man and the Thinker,* ed. Thomas Sheehan (Chicago: Precedent, 1981), p. 98.

13. F. Bradford Wallack, *The Epochal Nature of Process in Whitehead's Metaphysics* (Albany: State University of New York Press, 1980), p. 55.

14. John E. Smith, "Experience, Analogy and Religious Insight," in *Experience, Reason and God,* ed. Eugene Thomas Long (Washington, DC: Catholic University of America Press., 1980), p. 13.

15. Schrag, "Whitehead and Heidegger," p. 53.

16. Whitehead, *Adventures of Ideas,* p. 221.

CHAPTER TWO:

1. Schrag, "Phenomenology, Ontology, and History in the Philosophy of Heidegger," in *Phenomenology: The Philosophy of Edmund Husserl and Its Interpretation,* ed. Joseph J. Kockelmans (Garden City, NY: Doubleday, 1967), p. 289.

2. J. L. Mehta, *Martin Heidegger: The Way and the Vision* (Honolulu: University Press of Hawaii, 1976), pp. 46–47.

3. Magda King, *Heidegger's Philosophy: A Guide to His Basic Thought* (New York: Macmillan, 1964), pp. 160–61.

4. Edmund Husserl, *Ideas: General Introduction to Pure Phenomenology,* trans. W. R. Boyce Gibson (London: Collier-Macmillan, 1962), pp. 93–94.

5. While Dilthey's influence upon Heidegger is evident here, it must be pointed out that Heidegger's method allows him to escape the historical relativism that victimized Dilthey. Dilthey's thought is dependent upon the ontical use of categories, but Heidegger intends to overcome historical relativism through an ontological analysis of the meaning of historical possibility itself. See Heidegger's remarks on Dilthey and Yorck, BT 449–45.

6. Mehta, pp. 40–41.

7. Hans-Georg Gadamer, *Truth and Method,* translation copyright 1975 by Sheed and Ward (New York: Crossroad, 1984), p. 269.

8. Donald W. Sherburne, *A Key to Whitehead's "Process and Reality"* (Chicago: University of Chicago Press, 1981), p. 2. Quotation in Sherburne's passage is from OR xii.

9. Schrag, "Whitehead and Heidegger," p. 46.

10. Whitehead, *The Concept of Nature* (Cambridge: Cambridge University Press, 1964), p. 53.

11. Whitehead, *Science and the Modern World* (New York: Macmillan, 1925; rep. New York: Mentor Books, 1962), p. 87. Cf. PR 67.

12. Cf. Robert C. Neville, "Whitehead on the One and the Many," in *Explorations in Whitehead's Philosophy,* ed. Lewis S. Ford and George L. Kline (New York: Fordham University Press, 1987), pp. 257–71.

13. Kraus, p. 10.

14. Whitehead uses "actual entity" more often that "actual occasion." He says that while the terms are indeed synonymous, "actual occasion" better expresses certain features (PR 73, 77). I prefer the term "actual occasion" because it seems better to characterize the units of process as events rather than objects. To avoid confusion, Whitehead restricts the term "event" (though like many of his other technical terms, without total consistency) to a nexus, but with the reminder that "an actual occasion is the limiting type of an event with only one member" (PR 73).

15. George Santayana, *The Letters of George Santayana,* ed. David Cory (New York: Scribner's, 1955), letter to Mrs. C. H. Toy, p. 30.

1. In later works, Heidegger underscores this notion etymologically with a hyphen: *Ek-sistenz.*

2. Dreyfus and Dreyfus, pp. 28–29.

3. William J. Richardson, *Heidegger: Through Phenomenology to Thought* (The Hague: Martinus Nijhoff, 1967), p. 38. Cf. BT 120.

4. John Sallis, "Into the Clearing," in *Heidegger: The Man and the Thinker,* ed. Thomas Sheehan (Chicago: Precedent, 1981), pp. 109–10.

5. William A. Christian, *An Interpretation of Whitehead's Metaphysics,* (Westport, CN: Greenwood Press, 1959), p. 307.

6. Donald W. Sherburne, *A Whiteheadian Aesthetic: Some Interpretations of Whitehead's Metaphysical Speculation* (New Haven, CN: Archon Books, Yale University Press, 1961), p. 45.

7. Christian, p. 215.

8. Wallack, p. 121.

9. Ibid.

10. In "The Ramifications of Whitehead's Theory of Experience," *The Monist* (October 1985): 439–50, Lewis S. Ford (p. 439) says that "the phenomenological method makes two assumptions at odds with Whitehead's approach." The first assumption made by phenomenology is that "experience presupposes consciousness." Obviously, Ford does not

have Heidegger's version of the phenomenological method in mind. The second assumption is that "there is much to be gained by the recovery of 'pure' experience unencumbered by philosophical interpretation." While both Heidegger and Whitehead repudiate the first assumption that Ford attributes to phenomenology, they both accept the second assumption. Ford explains that since any examination of our experiences includes conscious interpretation, Whitehead would maintain that we can never reach "pure" experience. However, Ford seems not to appreciate the fact that for Whitehead, all experience is interpretative. Furthermore, we shall see in the following chapter on perception in the mode of causal efficacy that we do have available something like pure experiences.

11. Kraus, p. 31.

12. While God plays an important role in Whitehead's metaphysics, the notion is of no great importance to this study. Suffice it to say that given certain special features, God is more or less subject to all the categories that apply to other actual occasions. The prominence of God in Whitehead's thought marks an obvious contrast to that Heidegger, in spite of Heidegger's tremendous influence upon theology. Similarly, the Platonism inherent to the doctrine of eternal objects represents a extra-experiential realm unavailable to and unwelcome in Heidegger's phenomenology.

13. Whitehead also says that the doctrine of hybrid physical feelings contributes to the avoidance in the philosophy of organism of the "disastrous separation of body and mind" (PR 246).

14. Whitehead, *Adventures of Ideas,* p. 180.

15. Kraus, p. 4.

Chapter Four:

1. Schrag, *Experience and Being* (Evanston, IL: Northwestern University Press, 1969), p. 198.

2. Gadamer, *Truth and Method,* pp. 401, 402.

3. Joseph P. Fell, *Heidegger and Sartre: An Essay on Being and Place* (New York: Columbia University Press, 1979), p. 52.

4. James M. Demske, *Being, Man, and Death* (Lexington: University Press of Kentucky, 1981), pp. 55–56.

5. Alfonso Lingis, "Difference in the Eternal Recurrence of the Same," *Research in Phenomenology* 8 (1978): 78.

6. Zimmerman, *Eclipse of the Self,* p. 71.

7. Christian, p. 31.

8. A number of commentators have expressed their trouble with this term: e.g., Charles Hartshorne, "Whitehead's Novel Intuition," in *Alfred North Whitehead: Essays on His Philosophy,* ed. George L. Kline

(Englewood Cliffs, NJ: Prentice-Hall, 1963), p. 22; also, David R. Griffin comments on Hartshorne's criticism of perishing in "Hartshorne's Differences from Whitehead," in *Two Process Philosophers: Hartshorne's Encounter with Whitehead,* ed. Lewis S. Ford (Tallahassee, FL: American Academy of Religion, 1973), pp. 53–54.

9. Whitehead, *Science and Philosophy* (New York: Philosophical Library, 1948; repr. 1974), p. 126.

10. Mason, *Time and Providence,* p. 331.

11. Whitehead, *Adventures of Ideas,* p. 238.

12. Wallack, p. 163.

13. Whitehead, *Adventures of Ideas,* p. 191.

CHAPTER FIVE:

1. Mehta, p. 252.

2. Zimmerman, "The Unity and Sameness of the Self as Depicted in *Being and Time,*" *Journal of the British Society for Phenomenology* 6 (October 1975): 160.

3. Zimmerman, "Heidegger and Nietzsche on Authentic Time," *Cultural Hermeneutics* 4 (July 1977): 243.

4. David Couzens Hoy, "History, Historicity, and Historiology in *Being and Time,*" in *Heidegger and Modern Philosophy,* ed. Michael Murray (New Haven, CN: Yale University Press, 1978), p. 329.

5. Ibid., p. 340.

6. George Joseph Seidel, *Martin Heidegger and the Pre-Socratics* (Lincoln: University of Nebraska Press, 1964), p. 122.

7. Ibid.

8. Werner Marx, *Heidegger and the Tradition,* trans. Theodore Kisiel and Murray Greene (Evanston, IL: Northwestern University Press, 1971), p. 102.

9. Hoy, p. 341.

10. Zimmerman, *Eclipse of the Self,* p. 114.

11. Fell, *Heidegger and Sartre,* p. 64.

12. Michael Gelven, *A Commentary on Heidegger's "Being and Time"* (New York: Harper and Row, 1970), p. 203.

13. Christian, p. 81.

14. V. C. Chappell, "Whitehead's Theory of Becoming," in *Alfred North Whitehead: Essays on His Philosophy,* ed. George L. Kline (Englewood Cliffs, NJ: Prentice-Hall, 1963), pp. 70–80.

15. David A. Sipfle, "On the Intelligibility of the Epochal Theory of Time," *The Monist* 53 (1969): 505–18.

16. Wallack, pp. 249–50.

17. Ibid.

18. Whitehead is not always careful in distinguishing an actual occasion from a nexus. In a passage concerning Locke's notion of a particular thing, the reader may be led to think that crows and sheep are individual actual occasions (PR 53). Wallack appears to be led to such a view, and she lists a number of things (on pp. 28–29 of her book) that few other Whitehead scholars would agree are actual occasions; e.g., birds, trees, buildings, cities, histories of cultures, and the solar system. I think that Wallack is mistaken in explaining that Whitehead often does not distinguish actual occasions from nexūs "since an actual entity in any case composes a nexus of antecedent actual entities, and since any actual entity can be seen as a nexus of its component actual entities" (Wallack, p. 11).

19. Wallack, p. 176.
20. Kraus, p. 129.
21. Christian, p. 81.
22. Kraus, p. 76.
23. Whitehead, *Symbolism,* p. 129.
24. Kraus, p. 32 n. 29.
25. Whitehead, *Symbolism,* p. 43.

CHAPTER SIX:

1. However, the discoveries of quantum physics may suggest, says Charles Hartshorne, "important qualifications." See "Bell's Theorem and Stapp's Revised View of Space-Time," *Process Studies* 7 (Fall 1977): 183–91.

2. Kraus, p. 120.
3. Mehta, pp. 161–62.
4. Mason, p. 194.
5. Edward S. Casey, *Remembering,* p. 123.
6. Kraus, p. 151.

CHAPTER SEVEN:

1. A concept of authenticity is not readily found in Whitehead's book, but perhaps Whitehead's remarks on responsibility provide hints at such a concept. For example, he writes that "the actual entity, in a state of process during which it is not fully determinate, determines its own ultimate definiteness. This is the whole point of moral responsibility" (PR 255). See also the brief remarks in PR 47, 222, 224.

2. A similar description of holy experiences can be found in John E. Smith, "The Experience of the Holy and the Idea of God," in *Phe-*

*nomenology in America,* ed. James M. Edie (Chicago: Quadrangle Books, 1976), pp. 295–306. For example, Smith speaks of holy events as having "a capacity for calling attention to the being of the self and to life as a whole" (p. 299).

3. Ibid., p. 298.

4. Rudolph Otto, *The Idea of the Holy,* trans. John W. Harvey (New York: Oxford University Press, 1950), p. 6.

5. John A. T. Robinson, *Honest to God* (Philadelphia: Westminster Press, 1963), p. 87.

6. Ibid., p. 88.

7. Paul Tillich, *Dynamics of Faith* (New York: Harper and Row, 1957), p. 13.

8. Otto, p. 31.

9. Ernst Cassirer, *The Philosophy of Symbolic Forms,* vol. 2, *Mythical Thought* (New Haven: Yale University Press, 1955) p. 78.

10. Gadamer, pp. 132, 133: stress added.

11. Cassirer, p. 104.

12. Heidegger, *Poetry, Language, Thought,* trans. Albert Hofstadter (New York: Harper and Row, 1971), p. 31.

13. Smith, "Experience of the Holy," p. 301.

14. Whitehead, *Symbolism,* p. 27.

15. Whitehead, *An Enquiry Concerning the Principles of Natural Knowledge,* 2d ed. (New York: Dover, 1925; repr. 1982), p. 3.

CONCLUSION:

1. Whitehead, *Science and Philosophy,* p. 131.

2. Whitehead, *Enquiry Concerning Natural Knowledge,* p. 61.

3. Ibid.

4. Whitehead, *Science and Philosophy,* p. 122.

# Bibliography

Casey, Edward S. *Remembering: A Phenomenological Study.* Bloomington: Indiana University Press, 1987.

Cassirer, Ernst. *The Philosophy of Symbolic Forms,* vol. 2, *Mythical Thought.* New Haven, CN: Yale University Press, 1955.

Chappell, V. C. "Whitehead's Theory of Becoming." In *Alfred North Whitehead: Essays on His Philosophy,* pp. 70–80, edited by George L. Kline. Englewood Cliffs, NJ: Prentice-Hall, 1963.

Christian, William A. *An Interpretation of Whitehead's Metaphysics.* Westport, CN: Greenwood Press, 1959.

Demske, James M. *Being, Man, and Death.* Lexington: University Press of Kentucky, 1981.

Dreyfus, Hubert L., and Stuart E. Dreyfus. "Making a Mind Versus Modeling the Brain." *Daedalus* (Winter 1988): 20–43.

Fell, Joseph P. *Heidegger and Sartre: An Essay on Being and Place.* New York: Columbia University Press, 1979.

Ford, Lewis. "The Ramifications of Whitehead's Theory of Experience." *The Monist* (October 1985): 439–50.

Gadamer, Hans-Georg. *Truth and Method.* Translation copyright by Sheed and Ward Ltd., 1975. New York: Crossroad, 1984.

Gelven, Michael. *A Commentary on Heidegger's "Being and Time."* New York: Harper and Row, 1970.

Grene, Marjorie. *The Knower and the Known.* Berkeley: University of California Press, 1974.

Griffin, David R. "Hartshorne's Differences from Whitehead." In *Two Process Philosophers: Hartshorne's Encounter with Whitehead,* pp. 35–57, edited by Lewis S. Ford. Tallahassee, FL: American Academy of Religion, 1973.

Hartshorne, Charles. "Bell's Theorem and Stapp's Revised View of Space-Time." *Process Studies* 7 (Fall 1977): 183–91.

———. *Insights and Oversights of Great Philosophers.* Albany: State University of New York Press, 1983.

———. Review of *Being and Time. The Philosophical Review* 38 (1929).

———. "Whitehead's Novel Intuition." In *Alfred North Whitehead: Essays on His Philosophy,* pp. 18–26, edited by George L. Kline. Englewood Cliffs, NJ: Prentice-Hall, 1963.

Heidegger, Martin. *Being and Time.* Translated by John Macquarrie and Edward Robinson. New York: Harper and Row, 1962.

*147*

_____. *Poetry, Language, Thought.* Translated by Albert Hofstadter. New York: Harper and Row, 1971.

Hoy, David Couzens. "History, Historicity, and Historiology in *Being and Time.*" In *Heidegger and Modern Philosophy,* edited by Michael Murray. New Haven, CT: Yale University Press, 1978.

Husserl, Edmund. *Ideas: General Introduction to Pure Phenomenology.* Translated by W. R. Boyce Gibson. London: Collier-Macmillan, 1962.

King, Magda. *Heidegger's Philosophy: A Guide to His Basic Thought.* New York: Macmillan, 1964.

Kisiel, Theodore. "Towards a Topology of Dasein." In *Heidegger: The Man and the Thinker,* pp. 95–105, edited by Thomas Sheehan. Chicago: Precedent, 1981.

Kraus, Elizabeth M. *The Metaphysics of Experience: A Companion to Whitehead's "Process and Reality."* New York: Fordham University Press, 1979.

Lingis, Alphonso. "Difference in the Eternal Recurrence of the Same." *Research in Phenomenology* 8 (1978): 77–91.

Marx, Werner. *Heidegger and the Tradition.* Translated by Theodore Kisiel and Murray Green. Evanston, IL: Northwestern University Press, 1971.

Mason, David R. *Time and Providence: An Essay Based on an Analysis of the Concept of Time in Whitehead and Heidegger.* Washington, DC: University Press of America, 1982.

Mehta, J. L. *Martin Heidegger: The Way and the Vision.* Honolulu: University of Hawaii Press, 1976.

Neville, Robert C. "Whitehead on the One and the Many." In *Explorations in Whitehead's Philosophy,* pp. 257–71, edited by Lewis S. Ford and George L. Kline. New York: Fordham University Press, 1987.

Otto, Rudolf. *The Idea of the Holy.* Translated by John W. Harvey. New York: Oxford University Press, 1950.

Richardson, William J. *Heidegger: Through Phenomenology to Thought.* The Hague: Martinus Nijhoff, 1967.

Robinson, John A. T. *Honest to God.* Philadelphia: Westminster Press, 1963.

Sallis, John. "Into the Clearing." In *Heidegger: The Man and the Thinker,* pp. 107–15, edited by Thomas Sheehan. Chicago: Precedent, 1981.

Santayana, George. *The Letters of George Santayana.* Edited by David Cory. New York: Scribner's, 1955.

Schrag, Calvin O. *Existence and Freedom: Towards an Ontology of Human Finitude.* Evanston, IL: Northwestern University Press, 1970.

———. *Experience and Being.* Evanston, IL: Northwestern University Press, 1969.

———. "Phenomenology, Ontology, and History in the Philosophy of Heidegger." In *Phenomenology: The Philosophy of Edmund Husserl and Its Interpretation,* pp. 277-93, edited by Joseph J. Kockelmans. Garden City, NY: Doubleday, 1967.

———. "Whitehead and Heidegger: Process Philosophy and Existential Philosophy." *Dialectica* 13 (March 1959): 42-56.

Seidel, George Joseph. *Martin Heidegger and the Pre-Socratics.* Lincoln: University of Nebraska Press, 1964.

Sherburne, Donald W. *A Key to Whitehead's "Process and Reality."* Chicago: University of Chicago Press, 1981.

———. *A Whiteheadian Aesthetic: Some Interpretations of Whitehead's Metaphysical Speculations.* New Haven, CN: Archon Books, Yale University Press, 1961.

Sipfle, David A. "On the Intelligibility of the Epochal Theory of Time." *The Monist* 53 (1969): 505-18.

Smith, John E. "Experience, Analogy and Religious Insight." In *Experience, Reason and God,* pp. 5-18, edited by Eugene Thomas Long. Washington, DC: Catholic University of America Press, 1980.

———. "The Experience of the Holy and the Idea of God." In *Phenomenology in America,* pp. 295-306, edited by James M. Edie. Chicago: Quadrangle Books, 1976.

Spiegleberg, Herbert. *The Phenomenological Movement: A Historical Introduction.* The Hague: Martinus Nijhoff, 1965.

Tillich, Paul. *Dynamics of Faith.* New York: Harper and Row, 1957.

Wallack, F. Bradford. *The Epochal Nature of Process in Whitehead's Metaphysics.* Albany: State University of New York Press, 1980.

Whitehead, Alfred North. *Adventures of Ideas.* New York: Macmillan, 1933; rep., New York: Free Press, 1967.

———. *The Concept of Nature.* Cambridge: Cambridge University Press, 1964.

———. *An Enquiry Concerning the Principles of Natural Knowledge.* 2d ed. New York: Dover, 1925; rep. 1982.

———. *The Interpretation of Science: Selected Essays.* Edited by A. H. Johnson, New York: Bobbs Merrill, 1961.

———. *Modes of Thought.* New York: G. P. Putnam's Sons, 1958.

———. *Process and Reality: An Essay in Cosmology.* Corrected ed. by David Ray Griffin and Donald W. Sherburne. New York: Free Press, 1978.

———. *Science and the Modern World.* New York: Macmillan, 1925; rep., Mentor Books, 1962.

———. *Science and Philosophy.* New York: Philosophical Library, 1948; rep. 1974.

———. *Symbolism.* New York: Macmillan, 1927; rep., New York: Capricorn Books, 1959.

Zimmerman, Michael E. *Eclipse of the Self: The Development of Heidegger's Concept of Authenticity.* Athens: Ohio University Press, 1981.

———. "Heidegger and Nietzsche on Authentic Time." *Cultural Hermeneutics* 4 (July 1977): 239–64.

———. "The Unity and Sameness of the Self as Depicted in *Being and Time*." *Journal of the British Society for Phenomenology* 6 (October 1975): 157–67.

# A NOTE ABOUT THE AUTHOR

Ron Cooper is a native South Carolinian who received his Ph.D. in philosophy from Rutgers University. He currently lives with his wife in St. Petersburg where he is Resource Center Director for the Florida Humanities Council and occasionally teaches as an adjunct at colleges around the Tampa Bay area.